Neighborhood Girl

A MEMOIR OF LOSS, LONGING, AND LETTING GO

Linda Schifino

BROWN POSEY PRESS

an imprint of Sunbury Press, Inc.
Mechanicsburg, PA USA

an imprint of Sunbury Press, Inc.
Mechanicsburg, PA USA

Copyright © 2023 Linda Schifino.
Cover Copyright © 2023 by Sunbury Press, Inc.

Sunbury Press supports copyright. Copyright fuels creativity, encourages diverse voices, promotes free speech, and creates a vibrant culture. Thank you for buying an authorized edition of this book and for complying with copyright laws. Except for the quotation of short passages for the purpose of criticism and review, no part of this publication may be reproduced, scanned, or distributed in any form without permission. You are supporting writers and allowing Sunbury Press to continue to publish books for every reader. For information contact Sunbury Press, Inc., Subsidiary Rights Dept., PO Box 548, Boiling Springs, PA 17007 USA or legal@sunburypress.com.

For information about special discounts for bulk purchases, please contact Sunbury Press Orders Dept. at (855) 338-8359 or orders@sunburypress.com.

To request one of our authors for speaking engagements or book signings, please contact Sunbury Press Publicity Dept. at publicity@sunburypress.com.

FIRST BROWN POSEY PRESS EDITION: September 2023

Set in Adobe Garamond Pro | Interior design by Crystal Devine | Cover by Lawrence Knorr | Edited by Sarah Illick.

Publisher's Cataloging-in-Publication Data
Names: Schifino, Linda, author.
Title: Neighborhood girl : a memoir of loss, longing, and letting go / Linda Schifino.
Description: First trade paperback edition. | Mechanicsburg, PA : Brown Posey Press, 2023.
Summary: Linda Schifino's beloved childhood neighborhood is gone, family homes and church demolished, and family members long dead. Faced with heartbreaking loss, Schifino hoards treasured family memories and customs. When her son asks if it's okay to bring a ham to Christmas Eve Feast of the Seven Fishes, Schifino fears the dismantling of her family traditions.
Identifiers: ISBN : 979-8-88819-124-8 (paperback) | ISBN : 979-8-88819-125-5 (ePub).
Subjects: FAMILY & RELATIONSHIPS / General.

Product of the United States of America
0 1 1 2 3 5 8 13 21 34 55

For the Love of Books!

For Alex

For Alex

Contents

		Author's Note	*vii*
		Acknowledgments	*ix*
PART ONE		LIFE ON LARIMER	
	I	Empty Spaces	*3*
	II	Life on Larimer	*7*
	III	Fathers and Daughters	*16*
	IV	Running Numbers for Chocolate	*28*
	V	Baw Baw and the Saint Rocco Festival	*34*
	VI	My Other Mother	*40*
	VII	Bless Me, Father, for I Have Sinned	*48*
	VIII	Skipping Church	*58*
PART TWO		LIVING WITH LOSS	
	IX	Everything Changed	*65*
	X	Ursula	*70*
	XI	Neighborhood Boy	*74*
	XII	Norma and Dan	*83*
	XIII	Searching for the Sweetness	*92*
	XIV	Driving in Cars	*101*
	XV	Mim	*107*
	XVI	My Father's Hands	*111*
PART THREE		BEQUEATHING THE LEGACY	
	XVII	Three Fishes and a Ham	*119*
	XVIII	A Sign	*128*
	XIX	Decoration Day	*135*
	XX	Epilogue – Spaces Filled	*142*
		About the Author	*148*

Author's Note

The people, places, and events in the stories that follow are true to the very best of my recollection. That said, I acknowledge that memory is not infallible. I can only assure my readers that I have made every effort to remember each detail with as much accuracy as possible and that the essence of every story and event is true.

Acknowledgments

I am filled with gratitude for the friendship and support I received while writing *Neighborhood Girl*. Many thanks to my writer friends, especially the Madwomen in the Attic, who read early drafts, offering critique, good humor, and much support. Thanks to the Carlow University MFA community, both in Pittsburgh and Dublin, for providing excellent mentorships and residencies that inspired my writing—Tess Barry, Lou Boyle, Jan Beatty, Diane Glancy, Brian Leydon, and my good friend, the brilliant Joseph Bathanti who understands and shares my love for our Larimer Avenue heritage.

A special thanks to Gerry LaFemina, who read each draft of my manuscript with generosity and care, offering amazing insight, asking prodding questions, and providing unfailing support. I'm forever grateful to you, my dear friend.

I'm deeply appreciative of my family—my sister Tisha and my sons Sean and Jason, for their constant love and encouragement. I'm especially grateful for my dear granddaughter, Alex, who keeps me grounded, makes me laugh, and loves me unconditionally.

Versions of the following essays originally appeared in these publications: An excerpt from "Baw Baw and the Saint Rocco Festival" first appeared under the title "I Just Want to Hear Him Sing" in *Voices from the Attic*, VOL XXV, 2019. "Skipping Church" was published in *Adelaide Literary Magazine*, Issue 38, August 2020. "Running Numbers for Chocolate" appeared in *Northern Appalachia Review* in August 2021 (nominated for Best American Essays, 2021). "Searching for the Sweetness" was published in *Avalon Literary Review*, Winter, 2022

PART ONE
Life on Larimer

"Nothing is ever really lost to us as long as we remember it."
—Lucy Maud Montgomery, *The Story Girl*

1

Empty Spaces

Late on a July afternoon in 2017, I turned on impulse from Washington Boulevard onto Shetland Avenue and into the Larimer neighborhood where I was born and spent the first nine years of my life. I hadn't been to my old neighborhood in the East Liberty section of Pittsburgh in over thirty-five years, but Larimer Avenue had been on my mind. I had just celebrated a milestone birthday and had beat cancer a few years before, soon after the birth of my granddaughter. Childhood memories of that extraordinary time and place tugged at me. I wanted to go back. As I turned onto Shetland Avenue, I had no idea what to expect, and there was a feeling in the pit of my stomach somewhere between Christmas morning and a stress test.

"You're going where?" My sister, Tisha, asked when I called. "I really don't think you should be doing this alone. I remember hearing about street gangs and shootings."

"That was back in the nineties," I said with more confidence than I felt. "I'm sure it's fine now." Ten years younger, Tisha never lived on Larimer Avenue and didn't share—and perhaps couldn't understand—my intense need to make this journey. After all, she wasn't a neighborhood girl. She didn't live in the little three-room apartment over Mr. Corazza's grocery store; she didn't watch neighbors pass by as she played with her dolls on the front stoop; she didn't experience these places, know these people.

Tisha stayed on the phone while I started up Shetland through the intersection of Lincoln, then Lowell, then Winfield, watchful as I drove past houses in varying states of disrepair, sparsely dotting each side of the street. Some with peeling paint or sagging porch roofs, others looking abandoned, with broken windows and missing front doors. I noticed the occasional person sitting on a front porch, and they seemed to notice me as well. I continued down Shetland across Paulson and into the last long block approaching Larimer. The air conditioner was full blast, but my hands sweated on the steering wheel. I took a deep breath and made the right turn.

Grass stood knee-high on each side of the street, and small trees grew where the buildings of my childhood once stood.

"Oh, my God, Tisha, it's nothing but vacant lots!"

"Not any buildings at all?"

I glanced in the rearview mirror. "The school's still here, but it looks boarded up." I continued past the stretch of empty lots toward the last block before the Larimer Bridge—the block where I had lived. Crumbled concrete steps led to empty spaces; space that once held Mrs. Gentilcore's chicken store and the coal yard next door where I played covered in dust; space once occupied by the Italian Brotherhood Beneficial Association, where my great-grandfather drank too much and sang too loud; space where Ursula's beer store once stood directly across from our apartment.

One lone red brick building near the end of the block stood like a gallant soldier, the sole survivor of time and decay. My eyes were fixed on the storefront, the second-floor apartment windows, and the wooden back porch. I allowed myself to believe that it might be our apartment.

"It looks like maybe our building is here," My throat tightened, overwhelmed by the possibility. As I drove closer, it was clear this was not our building. It was Henry Grasso's sausage store, the last remnant of a lost neighborhood.

"I have to call you back." I pulled over, put my head on the steering wheel, and sobbed. I wept for all the lost buildings, the lost relatives and friends, and the lost memories that were just beyond my reach.

When I stopped crying and looked up, I faced the Larimer Avenue Bridge with its stone pillars at each side of the entrance. I pictured my dad and I strolling across, holding hands, laughing, and singing. I turned my gaze left down Orphan Street and recalled countless walks to my grandmother's house near the corner of Orphan and Whittier. I put my Honda in gear and drove there only to discover more broken concrete steps leading to a plot of weeds where Grandma's house had stood.

I circled back onto Larimer Avenue, toward the school, and parked in front. The opening that once framed the beautiful stained-glass front window was covered with graffiti-splattered plywood. The elegant stone arch over the entrance remained, sheltering a boarded front door where someone had painted "KNOW THYSELF." I pictured myself, a child of six or seven, walking through the building's entrance, strolling down its marble halls and up the grand staircase, belonging in this place. Across the street, the old club yard where kids once rode their bikes, the site of the Saint Rocco Festival each summer, and where I had performed in a school dance sat empty, its fence rusted, grass overgrown.

Thoughts of the Saint Rocco Festival invited memories of our church, so I drove further down Larimer and turned left onto Meadow Street. I pulled to the curb across the street from Our Lady Help of Christians, where my mother and I had attended Mass each Sunday. The large carved wooden doors were boarded up, weeds peeked out of crumbling steps, and the once magnificent stained-glass windows were now shattered into multi-colored shards. The grand domes survived but had lost their gold luster. The church that had nourished the souls of three generations of my family looked forsaken.

Afternoon was giving way to evening, but I needed to venture down Larimer Avenue again before heading home. I drove slowly this time, stopping on each block to mentally recreate the buildings, revisit old neighbors, and contemplate a childhood. I thought about the reality of a working poor community peppered with small-time criminals on street corners, immersed in the racism that characterized the 1950s, rooted in the struggles of immigrants who lived in tiny apartments and carried lunch pails to work—and the childhood that I embraced, idealized, loving, safe.

I was still a neighborhood girl.

Larimer School. (Source: Leepaxton at en.wikipedia, https://commons.wikimedia.org)

II

Life on Larimer

One of my early memories of life on Larimer Avenue was collecting soda bottles. My parents never bought soda—what we Pittsburghers call pop—as it was too expensive, but other folks in the neighborhood drank it, and they often discarded the bottles in the alley behind our building. I policed the alley, eyes peeled for the glint of glass, knowing that my mom was counting on me to collect enough bottles for her to make dinner.

From the time they were married until I was nine years old, my parents rented a small three-room apartment over a grocery store. Domenic Corazza owned the building and the store on the ground floor. My mother often sent me downstairs to pick up something she needed for dinner. When fresh tomatoes were scarce in the winter, we bought canned ones and a small container of tomato paste to make pasta sauce. I don't remember the price of most of the food in Mr. Corazza's store, but I know that a can of Contadina tomato paste cost fourteen cents. I usually paid for it with empty pop bottles. Mr. Corazza would credit two cents for each glass bottle, and I would drop off two or three at a time until I had seven, enough for tomato paste. Then, I'd climb the stairs to our second-floor apartment, where my mother waited in the kitchen.

Our kitchen was quite large, with a yellow Formica-topped table and matching chrome-legged chairs in the center. Faded tan linoleum with dull yellow spots that I'm guessing were once gold flecks covered the floor. One small window looked out into the narrow alley between our building and the one next door, and a brick fireplace took up most of the far wall next to the window. A sparrow flew down the chimney and into the kitchen one day, sending my mother screaming, so Dad closed the fireplace with a piece of plywood, rendering it useless.

The kitchen was the center of Mom's day—making scrambled eggs for breakfast, preparing the salad that we would eat after dinner each evening, and fixing sandwiches to pack in Dad's lunch for the next day. The kitchen table was also where Mike the peddler opened his brown paper sack, unfolding tea towels, pillowcases, and colorful housedresses that Mom held up to her shoulders, appraising the fit. After any purchases, I watched Mike, fascinated as he wrapped the sack in brown paper and re-tied the cord with a flick of his wrist. In the afternoon, Mom often relaxed at the kitchen table, sipping coffee with my Aunt Mim, while I sat on the floor playing with my dolls and listening to Patty Page on the portable record player singing "How Much Is That Doggie in the Window?"

A wide archway led from the kitchen into a cramped living room with an old-fashioned mohair sofa the color of rust and a small wooden coffee table one of my mom's older sisters gave us. By the time I was a toddler, our living room also sported a black and white television with a fifteen-inch screen surrounded by an oversized wooden cabinet. Dad maneuvered the rabbit ear antennae to bring in all three channels. I usually spent Saturday mornings sitting on the worn living room carpet in front of the TV watching *Howdy Doody* or *Sky King*, who used his plane, the *Songbird*, for thrilling rescue missions. I was jealous of his niece, Penny, who sometimes flew along. I imagined my dad and me high in the clouds, the two of us off to capture villains as he taught me how to fly the plane. Exciting daydreams, for sure. Yet, truth be told, I preferred the security of sitting grounded on our living room floor.

I stayed up late watching the *Friday Night Fights*, curled up on the sofa beside my dad. While he liked Joe Lewis and Sugar Ray Robinson, Dad's favorite was Rocky Marciano, the heavyweight champ with a powerful punch and durable chin. It didn't hurt that he was Italian. No matter who wore the gloves in the ring, Dad was fully engaged in the event. Once the bell sounded for the first round, Dad leaned forward in his seat, offering his critique. "Look at that. He's just holding on. He wants to dance, not fight. He's just a palooka."

I didn't much enjoy seeing Rocky Marciano and Jersey Joe Walcott pummel each other, but my dad loved boxing, and I adored my dad, so I just closed my eyes during the parts when the blood squirted.

Off the living room was an even smaller room where my parents and I slept. Mom and Dad shared the large bed, and I slept in a metal folding cot that sat against the front wall under the window. In the morning, Mom folded the cot with the thin mattress inside and latched it at the top like a piece of baloney between two slices of bread. The cot had wheels on the bottom so Mom could push it to the corner of the room out of the way. She called it a "roll away bed."

My Aunt Mim—Mom's closest of her five sisters—and Uncle Felix lived in a similar flat in the rear of our building. I thought Mim had the nicer place since she had a back porch off her kitchen. Childless, Mim, and Uncle (I dropped "Felix" because he was my favorite) were like my second parents. I sometimes ate meals with them, spent summer evenings on their back porch with Uncle and Dad listening to Rosey Rosewall announce the play-by-play for the Pirate games, and curled up in Uncle's lap for a reading of *Henry* in the Sunday comics. The doors to both apartments were usually left ajar, and I navigated back and forth, considering the entire second floor my home, enjoying the luxury of having four parents.

Our apartment faced the front of the building overlooking the street, and I liked to stand on my cot and take in the view of Larimer Avenue below. In the summer, when the windows were open, I could hear passing cars, the chatter of people on the sidewalk, friends greeting each other, and Mr. Corazza's door opening and closing as neighbors came and went from the grocery store below.

Mr. Corazza, a widower in his fifties who somehow seemed older, lived in an apartment behind the store with his two daughters, Nayda and Anita. The Corazza daughters, who were in their late teens when I was born, worked in the store after school. The girls fussed over me like I was one of the Precious Toddler dolls that were so popular back then, and I relished the attention.

Less animated than his daughters, Mr. Corazza didn't talk much, but when he spoke, it was with a pleasant Italian accent. He was taller than most of the immigrants in our neighborhood, and he had wiry grey hair brushed neatly off his forehead and bushy eyebrows that curved like canopies over his deep-set dark eyes. He had a prominent nose and generous lips that broadened into a tender smile when any neighborhood children entered the store.

Most of the time, Mr. Corazza sat on a wooden stool behind a long counter, slightly hunched over a large brown ledger book. Customers gathered what they needed—Giganti's Italian bread and cans of Folgers coffee from the shelves, cartons of milk and eggs from the cooler, and peaches and green beans from the crates outside on the sidewalk in the summer. Then, they'd stack their purchases on the counter in front of Mr. Corazza. He thumbed through the dog-eared ledger book until he came to that customer's page and recited their name: Ciorra, Martone, Martinelli, Schifino. He held each item in his thick, calloused hand and carefully recorded its description and price before he placed it in a paper bag. There was no exchange of money, no invoice, no discussion of what was owed. Just Mr. Corazza's "okay" as he handed over the sack of groceries.

On payday, neighborhood housewives came to settle their accounts. "How much do I owe, Mr. Corazza?" No one ever questioned the amount. Customers paid what they could, often only a fraction of the bill. "I'll add more next payday," they'd promise. The page with our name at the top always had a balance due. Yet, my mother was fastidious about the rent. At the beginning of every month, I'd accompany Mom downstairs to pay Mr. Corazza—in full, on time, in cash. I watched as she handed over the money, and Mr. Corazza put it in a zippered leather pouch. He didn't count it, and Mom never insulted him by asking for a receipt.

Next door to our building was the Italian Brotherhood Beneficial Association, or what we called the IBBA, where elderly men socialized over glasses of red wine and prosciutto sandwiches. I'd never been inside, nor had my parents that I know of, but my great-grandfather was a regular. Day and night, a group of men usually hung out on the sidewalk in front. I wondered why they weren't at work like my dad. Sometimes late on summer nights when it was warm, the men from the IBBA moved their drinking and loud banter onto the street. When we could hear their racket spilling through the open windows of our apartment, I'd watch my father get out of bed, put on his slippers, and march downstairs in his pajamas, ignoring my mother's pleas.

"Just wait a few minutes, Dan. They'll stop soon."

Dad was never gone long, and by the time he returned, the noise had ended, and we all drifted back to sleep.

Henry Grasso's store was next to the IBBA. Grasso's sold fresh meats, specializing in cuts from the pig—cured ham, homemade Italian sausage, and the less common parts like pig knuckles, feet, and tripe. Links of sausage and hams hung in the storefront window, olives soaked in brine in large barrels just inside the front door, and the floor was covered with sawdust that we kids enjoyed kicking around. On busy Saturday mornings, the buzz of shoppers almost drowned out the whirr of the meat grinder. Mr. Grasso worked behind the glass case at a butcher's table, cutting whole pigs into spareribs, loins, and pancetta. A large plastic pig was affixed to the wall over his shoulder as though it was overseeing Mr. Grasso's handiwork. The pork had no odor, so the entire store smelled of a mixture of spicy olive brine and the woodsy aroma of the sawdust. Mr. Grasso didn't keep a ledger, and you needed cash to make purchases. Sometimes my mom would ignore her grocery budget and buy one of the small jars of pickled pig's feet that sat on top of the meat case as a treat for my dad, who liked to eat them with garlic, red onion, and a chunk of crusty Italian bread.

Mr. and Mrs. Gentilcore owned the building next to Henry Grasso, where they ran a chicken store on the first floor and lived in an apartment on the second floor with their son Johnny and daughter Terry. Live chickens were delivered through the alley in the rear, where Mr. Gentilcore slaughtered and butchered them. Mrs. Gentilcore sold whole chickens and chicken parts to neighborhood housewives in the storefront. The Gentilcores also owned the vacant lot between their building and Grasso's, where they ran a modest coal business. On chilly fall days, local men arrived with wheelbarrows, which they loaded to keep their furnaces fueled over the winter. Then, they stuck their head in the front door of the chicken store, and Mrs. Gentilcore would come out. She'd examine the coal in the wheelbarrow and estimate the cost. There was no scale, so Ange Gentilcore applied her experienced eye. Sometimes one of the neighborhood men questioned her. "Are you sure, Angie? That seems like a lot." After some haggling, the transactions were completed.

Sometimes I played in the side yard with Mrs. Gentilcore's niece, Linda, who was my age and for a while lived with her aunt and uncle after her mother died. In the summer, Linda and I played hopscotch or jacks; we'd play in the coal piles in the fall. Playing with Linda allowed me to occasionally glimpse Johnny Gentilcore, a few years older and the object of my crush. Johnny was trim and athletic, with brown hair combed back in a pompadour and a wide, crooked smile that charmed me. I'd spot him from my perch on a pile of coal as he ran up his back porch steps, and I'd call hello, but Johnny ignored me.

Sometimes Linda's cousin Lois came to play with us. Lois lived in a suburb called Penn Hills and was the only kid I played with that didn't live in my neighborhood. While Linda and Lois were my age, they seemed tougher and more worldly, as though they knew things about life, about the neighborhood, that I didn't. Linda and Lois weren't bound to the same set of commandments that my mother handed down to me. They played outside as long as they liked without checking in, crossed the street without an adult, and were empowered with independence far beyond what I was allowed. I felt intimidated by them. Linda made a game of climbing up and running down the mountains of coal. I hated getting dirty, but I tolerated playing the game. It didn't take long for our hands, shoes, and clothes to get covered with black coal dust, and I'd feel the need to go home and wash. I was embarrassed to admit my compulsion for cleanliness, so I made excuses. "I have to go to the bathroom" was my usual pretext. I sensed they knew it was a fib but went along anyway.

One fall afternoon, when I was about seven or eight, the three of us walked up Larimer Avenue to Allen's 5 & 10. We had to cross two streets, which violated my mom's rules, but I didn't want to seem like a baby, so I didn't say anything. We entered the store and strolled through the aisles, looking at baby dolls, notebooks, and hair bands. I spied a pink eraser and thought about how it would make a nice addition to my pencil box. I picked it up and ran my fingers over the smooth rubber edges. I lifted it to my nose and savored the new eraser smell. I had no money and was about to replace the eraser in its slot when Linda and Lois spotted me.

"Just put it in your pocket," Linda said. "I'll look out so no one will see."

I was terrified. I really wanted the eraser, but I had never stolen anything before. I balanced my fear of getting caught against my anxiety about being humiliated in front of Linda and Lois. I knew they would tease me if I wasn't bold and didn't have the nerve to steal. I looked up and down the aisle and saw no other customers, so I slipped the eraser into my pocket and quickly left the store. There was no rush of adrenaline, no thrill, just relief to have made it safely outside. I felt uncomfortable, remorseful walking home, and disappointed that Linda and Lois didn't mention my courage. Ultimately, the experience didn't initiate me into stealing. I don't remember what I did with the eraser, but I still remember the feel and smell of it. And the guilt. I still remember the guilt, which couldn't be erased.

My mother's friend, Ursula, ran her beer store on the corner of Larimer and Orphan, directly across the street from our building. Looking out my bedroom window, I had a direct view of the comings and goings in the store. Some days, I stopped with my mom to say a quick hello to Ursula. Inside, the store's walls were lined with coolers holding six-packs of Iron City, Pabst Blue Ribbon, and Rolling Rock. The beer store was a one-person operation, with Ursula stocking the cooler, waiting on customers, and managing the cash register. If a customer wanted to buy an entire case, Ursula descended the narrow basement stairs and returned, balancing the case of beer on her shoulder, the muscles in her arms bulging under its weight. The large storefront window displayed bottles of the different types of beer sold inside, along with a light-up sign that spelled "Budweiser" that shone in my window at night.

My mother, who made friends easily and kept them for a lifetime, befriended Ursula when most neighbors seemed to keep their distance. Ursula was different. I assumed she was a woman because she wore skirts, had a woman's name, and everyone referred to her as "she." Yet, Ursula had a flat chest and the stubble of facial hair, and she had muscles in her arms, almost like my dad's. My parents didn't drink, so we never bought anything in the beer store, but my mother stopped in to see Ursula most days to say hello and sometimes to invite her to have dinner with my family. Ursula always declined, but she smiled in a way that said she was glad for the invitation.

Ursula drove an old black cargo van that she used to deliver beer. She named it "Chooch." After deliveries, Ursula let me ride along to put Chooch in the garage she rented a few streets away. Chooch rumbled along, and as I sat on the cracked leather seat, I felt each bump in the street. When we got to the garage, I stood in the alley while Ursula pulled Chooch inside and closed the large creaking garage doors. It was our evening ritual, and we called it "putting the Chooch to bed." Then we'd walk the few blocks to my building with my small hand enveloped in hers, somehow comforted by Ursula's calloused, rough skin. We'd turn on Orphan Street, passing small clapboard houses with flowerpots and swept front walks, and Urs would ask me about my day.

"I fell when I was on my skates in front of Mr. Grasso's store."

"Did you get hurt?"

"No, I'm ok."

"Good." Ursula squeezed my hand.

When we crossed Larimer Avenue and arrived at my building, Ursula would watch from below as I climbed the stairs to our apartment and my waiting mother.

My grandmother lived just two blocks from Ursula's store and around the corner on Whittier Street. Grandma raised ten children in that house, which was ironic since she had been an only child. I never knew my grandfather, who died long before I was born, but my great-grandfather, Baw Baw, lived with Grandma. On Sundays, we spent the day at Grandma's, her house overflowing with aunts, uncles, and cousins. We kids played in the small backyard between the tomato plants and flowers and chased each other through the house and out to the front porch. At dinner time, we ate Grandma's homemade cavatelli and freshly baked Italian bread. The adults crowded around Grandma's large dining room table, and my cousins and I sat in the kitchen at a porcelain-topped metal table with hinged leaves to accommodate all of us.

Grandma's kitchen was my favorite spot in her house. Grandma, her wavy grey hair piled in a bun clipped with bobby pins, always a white apron, always wearing stockings with her black open-toed shoes, standing at the six-burner stove where a pot of pasta sauce simmered all Sunday afternoon. I can still conjure up the smells of Grandma's kitchen—the pungent aroma of garlic sizzling in olive oil in a cast iron pan, the trace of basil fresh from the garden as Grandma tore it into pieces, the strong scent of Baw Baw's cigars encroaching on and mingling with the food smells. Sitting at the kitchen table, I could hear my aunts' and uncles' laughter spilling from the dining room and opera arias streaming from the old Victrola in the living room—the sounds of comfort, of home.

After dinner, Mom, Dad, and I walked with Mim and Uncle the two blocks back to our apartment. We passed Ursula's, with the Budweiser sign casting a light on the sidewalk in front of the darkened store. We approached our building, where Mr. Corazza had drawn the blinds in his storefront windows and brought the crates of vegetables and fruits inside. Larimer Avenue was quiet.

Folks in my neighborhood stayed for generations. They seemed oblivious to the post-war sprawl to the suburbs, or maybe scarcity kept them there. Scarcity of transportation since almost no one I knew owned a car and scarcity of funds to make a move affordable. Scarcity of options. Yet, as a child, I didn't see anything but abundance emanating from these people, these spaces. Their shared stories, history, and culture suggested a choice made by generations of families to stay in this Italian American enclave where trust and the warmth of community seemed to thrive. I'm glad they stayed. Larimer Avenue exists at the core of my identity, defining my childhood and shaping my future, the pulse of it still beating within me.

III

Fathers and Daughters

My son carried his four-year-old sleeping daughter to the car, holding her close. He carefully secured my granddaughter in her car seat, softly brushed her hair from her eyes, and closed the car door. Watching Sean and Alex reminded me of my father, and how I imagine he held me with the same care and attention. My father's hands were strong and steady, the hands of a working man. Yet sometimes, they tenderly enveloped my small ones; sometimes, they clapped with joy; other times they created animal shapes on the wall. Most often, Dad's hands sheltered me from the world, or at least tried to.

* * *

Some important things happened in the summer of 1953 when I was six. Dr. Jonas Salk was testing his polio vaccine with optimistic results. I overheard neighbors in Mr. Corazza's store talking about the rise of polio cases; panicked, they decided to keep their children away from crowded movie theaters and swimming pools. Salk's vaccine offered some hope for a cure. For my mother, the excitement came in early June with the coronation of Queen Elizabeth II. Mom watched the broadcast live from Westminster Abby on our black-and-white television as the young princess was crowned Queen of the United Kingdom. For my father, the most important topic of the summer was that the Pittsburgh Pirates traded their star homerun hitter, Ralph Kiner, to the Chicago Cubs. Dad was outraged, vowing for the first of many times that he'd "stop following the bums."

For me, the main event was my dad teaching me how to ride a bike. Being my father's daughter meant lots of protection, often at the expense of adventure. I wondered if this summer might be different. Yet, I was torn between the desire to learn to ride a bike and the fear of getting hurt. What if I fell? I wasn't used to engaging in anything risky. Dad had trained me to be cautious.

I got the hand-me-down bike from Dad's boss, Mr. Medica, who had two daughters older than me and had also given me skates and a toy piano. Once they sent me a tennis racket, which was strange since I didn't know anyone who played tennis, and I had no idea where a tennis court could be found. The bike was a welcome gift, but I wondered where I would ride it. I wasn't allowed beyond my block of Larimer Avenue without an adult, but perhaps I could travel the three doors up the street to Mrs. Gentilcore's coal yard. Maybe I'd ride in the alley behind our building and collect glass bottles in my basket. Maybe Mom would walk me and the bike to Grandma's so I could ride on the sidewalk in front of her house with my cousin Tommy.

The bike had a bright blue frame and a wide wire basket attached to the handlebars. I stood beside the bike while Dad inspected it and announced it was the right size. We stored it on Mim's back porch until the weekend when Dad and I would go out for my first ride. On Saturday morning, Dad retrieved the bike from the back porch, walked it through the second-floor hallway, and carried it down the steps, through the front door, and onto the street. I followed closely, eager to start. Dad pushed the bike along the sidewalk, past the doorway to Mr. Corazza's store, and started up Larimer Avenue towards the school.

"Why can't I ride, Daddy?"

"Not on the sidewalk. Not yet," he replied.

I walked beside Dad with the bike three blocks to Larimer School, trying to be patient. When we came to a cross street, Dad pushed the bike with one hand and reached for mine with the other, clutching it tightly until we crossed and reached the safety of the sidewalk. We arrived at the school, and Dad walked the bike inside the wrought iron gates onto the cracked asphalt schoolyard. The realization set in; I'm going to ride a two-wheel bicycle! A few other kids in the neighborhood, mostly boys, had bikes that they rode in the large club yard across the street from the school. I thought about how I might join them once I got good enough and how impressed everyone would be seeing me on my bright blue bicycle, riding in the club yard with the big kids. Dad reached down to adjust the training wheels so that they were ever so slightly above the ground.

"Okay," he said. "You can get on now."

I straddled the bicycle and sat on the narrow, padded seat. Dad showed me how to put my scuffed brown play shoes on the pedals and where to put my hands on the handlebars. All the while, his hands continued to grip the bike frame. Finally, he let go, and I pedaled away. I wasn't going fast enough to create wind in my hair, but I felt free. Still, it was a compromised freedom that felt both exhilarating and frightening. The front wheel jerked right and left as I twisted the handlebars each way to keep the bike moving forward. Dad ran just a few steps behind me as I circled the school yard. "Be careful," he yelled. I turned to look at him over my shoulder, and he yelled again. "Linda! Be careful!"

I made my way through the schoolyard, circling the building. The training wheels kept me upright, and I quickly mastered steering the handlebars to keep the bike straight. Still, Dad continued to run behind me. He followed closely behind every Saturday through that summer and into the fall, but he never agreed to lift the training wheels completely, and I never did learn to ride well enough to graduate to the club yard. By the following spring, I had forgotten about the bike. I'm not sure what ever happened to it.

***

Alex got her first two-wheel bike for her fourth birthday. One afternoon, I pulled up in front of my son's apartment building to find him and Alex on the sidewalk. She was perched on the seat of a bright blue bike while Sean buckled the strap of a pink helmet under her chin. Alex let go of the handlebars to wave to me as I got out of the car, and Sean calmly reminded her that she needed to hold on. I noticed the training wheels and smiled to myself. Alex rode the bike down the sidewalk toward the park at the end of their street, Sean and I following, giving her space.

"Keep going, Alex. You're doing a good job," Sean yelled. "Pretty soon, we'll get rid of those training wheels." Sean seemed to understand how to balance the tension between holding his daughter and holding her back.

***

My dad's concern for my safety was likely a byproduct of his unstable childhood. My father was orphaned when he was ten. His mom died in the spring of 1919 during the third wave of the influenza pandemic when Dad was only two. Presumably, his father couldn't work and care for his four children, so my dad was shuffled between relatives and boarding houses. I looked recently at the 1920 Pittsburgh census online and found the house where my father was a three-year-old boarder. It was a household of people with names I had never heard. I tried to picture my father as a toddler, thought of my own children at that age, and wondered if Dad was afraid, lonely, and confused. I ached to gather him in my arms, stroke his hair, nuzzle my face in his neck, and whisper, "It's okay. I'll take care of you."

Dad's father died eight years later after a work accident causing internal injuries. He was a teamster who drove a wagon led by two horses through Schenley Park, and a horse had kicked him in the stomach.

"He didn't get it taken care of, and it killed him," Dad said.

Some years later, when I discovered my grandfather's death certificate, it indicated a puncture of his abdominal wall, and he died of peritonitis just days after the incident.

Once both parents were gone, Dad lived with his twenty-year-old brother Nick, and his fifteen-year-old sister, Irene. Nick had a job with the city, and Irene kept house, but money was scarce, and there wasn't always enough to eat. Dad told stories of stealing food from the bins lining the sidewalk outside the local grocery store. "I'd grab whatever I could, potatoes, beans, fruit. Then I'd run like hell."

"You never got caught?" I asked.

Dad's face tightened, and his mouth formed a thin line. "One day, I was walking across the street from the grocery store, waiting for the right time to move in. All of a sudden, the owner of the store shows up in the doorway. He has this big basket filled with vegetables, fruit, and a loaf of Italian bread on top. 'Danny,' he yells to me. 'I made this basket for you.' I put my head down, pretended not to hear him, and got the hell out of there."

"Why didn't you take the groceries, Daddy?"

"There was no way I was taking a handout," he said.

I had heard stories before about my father stealing, usually from shopkeepers—food, clothes, and a pair of tennis shoes because he wasn't allowed to take gym class in his socks. Somehow, these petty crimes never seemed inconsistent with the honesty that characterized his adult life and that he demanded from me. I saw Dad as absolved. He was an orphan, after all.

Sometimes Dad ate meals with his Uncle Frank and Aunt Anna, who had four children of their own and limited funds. Dad described how Anna would pass around a plate of meat at dinner, first to her husband and next to her children, then last to him. Dad explained that most times, there wasn't any meat left. "I didn't mind," he said. "She had to worry about her own kids." As an adult, I noticed how Dad ate his meals hunched over his plate, his right hand grasping his fork, left arm spread on the table surrounding his plate, protecting his food.

Dad liked to tell the story of how he also stole from the local bootlegger. As Dad told it, "The bootlegger paid us neighborhood kids a couple of pennies for each empty bottle we brought him. So, I'd crawl into his basement window late at night and steal bottles off the shelves. Then, I'd wait a couple of days and show up at his front door to turn the bottles in for money. The damn fool didn't know his own bottles!" Dad laughed at each telling of the story. It reminded me of how I collected pop bottles in the alley behind our Larimer Avenue apartment.

Dad was twelve when the great depression made what seemed unbearable even worse. He spent his teenage years mostly on the street, so it wasn't surprising that his health failed. Dad was nineteen when he was diagnosed with tuberculosis after an unceasing cough that never improved. I was a teenager myself when I learned about it.

A cold that lasted a few weeks left me with a nagging cough. I overheard my parents arguing about whether I needed to visit a doctor, Mom insisting that it was not serious and Dad repeating, "You don't know that for sure."

Later, when I asked Mom why Dad was so concerned about a simple cold, she shared the story of his tuberculosis. I wanted to take it away, to re-write history so that it never happened. The injustice of adding tuberculosis to the list of Dad's misfortunes made me want to yell out in rage at the universe. Instead, I ran sobbing to my room.

Treatment for tuberculosis in the 1930s was limited. Without a cure or medication, doctors used a process that cut off the nerve supply to the diaphragm and another procedure where the infected lung was collapsed in the hopes that it would heal. Dad remembered the procedures and related them to me years later. "I had to be awake, so I wouldn't move," he said. "They used needles and burned the nerves. I could actually smell the burning." He related the story matter-of-factly, without bitterness or resentment, as though he was talking about someone else. I was horrified. It occurred to me then that Dad's collapsed lung was the cause of his right shoulder leaning lower than the left. It's funny how I never really noticed it until I understood the reason for it, and I wondered what else I hadn't noticed about Dad.

My father's early life struggles caused him always to seem anxious anytime there was a chance that I could be hurt or at risk. Maybe this explains why I can't ride a bike to this day, why I fear the water and never learned to swim, and why I'm afraid of heights. At the time, I didn't feel cheated. The sanctuary of Dad's care was worth any adventure I might have missed. Yet, when I entered high school at age thirteen, and my world expanded a bit, I realized what I had given up. I couldn't swim, so when my friends and I went to the Willows pool, I sat on my blanket as far away from the edge as possible. I was terrified that one of the boys would throw me in the water like they did in a playful and flirtatious way with my girlfriends. I couldn't join my friends bike riding to Highland Park or each other's houses. I made the excuse that I didn't have a bike, which was true, but I knew that access to a bike had little to do with being left out. I began to grasp the price I had paid for Dad's protection. The memory of Dad and me in the schoolyard with my first bike remained strong and deep-seated even though I had no recollection, or concern for that matter, about what happened to the bike. I came to recognize that this memory revealed an acceptance of my father's overprotection, acknowledging that he was not the perfect parent after all.

Dad seemed more at ease helping me with my homework, like when he and I made a solar system diorama for a school science project. A shoebox, a metal tin of colored paints, a pair of small scissors, and a glass bottle of Elmer's Glue-all with the silly-looking cow face on the front were spread out on newspaper that Mom gave us to protect the kitchen table. Dad cut the nine planets in appropriately varying sizes out of white construction paper, and I painted them. I finished the yellow Sun and the blue Earth and carefully applied bright red paint to the tiny circle representing Mercury. I watched Dad's large hands—tanned from working outdoors in the city parks yet immaculate with neatly trimmed nails—maneuver inside the shoe box to glue the small paper planets to pieces of thin wire stretched out connecting each planet to the Sun. Dad had created the universe for me to behold. Yet, it was contained in a tight box that epitomized the confines of my real world.

Dad taught me to read when I started Kindergarten, first by reading aloud and then helping me sound out the words he printed in block letters on a large, lined pad. He also taught me to write my name in upper and lower case letters. By the time I was in first grade, my skills were so advanced that my teacher and school principal convinced my parents to move me into second grade.

Dad also recognized the importance of critical thinking skills and taught me Scrabble, checkers, and chess. Sometimes after dinner, I'd get out the checkered board and the small cardboard box of red and black checkers from the closet shelf in my parents' bedroom and carry them to the kitchen table. "Can we play, Daddy?" I'd ask, plopping the checkers in front of him. I'm guessing there were times that Dad preferred to read his paper or to relax in front of the TV, but he never refused. He also didn't let me win, which made me feel more grown up. Over the years, I got better at the game, but there were only a few times I could beat him.

***

Alex smiled into the laptop's camera, and I realized how much I missed seeing her face unmasked. During that first winter of COVID, our video calls had replaced the outside, socially distanced visits from summer, which had replaced the previous six years of playing on my office floor, sharing breakfast after a sleep-over, cuddling on the sofa with Shel Silverstein's poems. I longed for her physical presence.

"I know how all the chess pieces move," Alex said proudly. "Daddy taught me." Her little fingers drew shapes on the computer screen. "The knight moves like a number seven, and the bishop moves on a diagonal in all the directions. The pawns can only go one way."

"Which is the most valuable piece?" I asked.

Alex thought for a bit. "Well, the queen can do anything she wants. But I guess the king is most valuable because if you get him, you win the game."

"Have you won any games?" I asked.

"Not yet. Daddy usually wins, but I'm going to win pretty soon. Daddy said that I'm getting better because I'm a good thinker."

* * *

One night, Dad and I had just put the checkers away, and he was tucking me into my cot when we heard the loud screech of a car outside. Mom left the kitchen where she was cleaning up, and the three of us went to the bedroom window overlooking Larimer Avenue. A man had been hit by a car right in front of our building. A crowd of neighbors quickly assembled, and I heard someone yell that they were calling for an ambulance. Mom ran outside to investigate while Dad and I stayed in the apartment. I stood on my cot, and Dad knelt behind me with his arm around me and his hand resting on my shoulder. We leaned on the windowsill, watching as police cars with flashing lights filled the street below, followed by an ambulance screaming its siren. I wasn't afraid, but I was glad that Dad was beside me—close enough to smell his Old Spice aftershave, close enough to lean against his chest.

When the ambulance arrived, Dad decided that we had seen enough, and he reached for one of the little Golden Books from the wall shelf behind me. As I lay on the cot, Dad read to me, and I half listened but kept my ears perked to the noises outside. The sounds of vehicles and people faded, and our street resumed its usual rhythm. But Mom didn't return.

After a while, Mim came through our apartment door and into the bedroom.

"Norma rode to the hospital in the ambulance," she told Dad. "She wanted to see what happened to the guy who was hit by that car."

Dad just shook his head with a smile, knowing that Mom couldn't resist excitement. My mom always had an intense fear of missing out. Dad sometimes teased her that she should have been a lawyer so she could make money chasing ambulances or fire trucks. While Dad couldn't stifle Mom's desire for excitement, he could, and did, stifle mine. Yet, I was content in Dad's protective care.

I settled into my cot, and Dad sat beside me until I fell asleep. I was awakened later by my mother's voice from the kitchen telling Dad that she got a ride home in one of the police cars. Mom was disappointed, however, that she couldn't discover details about the man's fate. While her curiosity remained unsatisfied, at least Mom fulfilled her need to be involved in the event so that she could talk about it with some authority to Mim and the neighbors the next day.

I slept in my cot for another year or so. Then, when I was seven, I came home from school one afternoon to find a new sofa in the living room. We weren't a family that bought new things. Our furniture was well-worn and secondhand, mostly given to my mom by her older siblings. So, a new sofa was a very big deal.

I stared at the modern light green couch that looked so out of place in our small living room, like a fancy lady who came to visit. My mother explained that the sofa was a pull-out bed where I would sleep. "We'll open it up every night, and it will already have sheets on it," she said. "We'll just bring in your pillow from our room." I had been sleeping in a fold-out cot since I left the crib, so sleeping on a sofa didn't concern me. I was used to pretend beds.

The pull-out sofa introduced a new bedtime routine. Since my parents wanted to watch TV or talk in the living room, I started in their bed, where I could stretch my arms and legs and roll over from one side to the other. But my parents' bed was a less exciting space. From my cot under the window, I could hear activity from Larimer Avenue. I liked feeling close to its energy, and I wondered if I would still feel connected to the street below while sleeping in my parents' bed.

Mom tucked me in after my prayers most nights, saying, "Go right to sleep, and Daddy will come in later to carry you to the sofa."

Eventually, I fell asleep, only to wake each morning in my sofa bed. When I opened my eyes, I could see through the archway into the kitchen where my mother would usually be at the stove making breakfast. Dad would be getting ready for work, collecting his lunch box and thermos, then sitting on the living room chair bent over, tying his work boots. I'd sit at the end of the sofa bed watching him until Dad came over to kiss me goodbye. "Have a good day, babe."

One Saturday early in May, Dad took me to work with him. It was the first day of May Market at Mellon Park, and Dad was responsible for preparing, raising tents, and ensuring that the walled garden and fountain area were pristine. I walked through the rows of tents behind Dad, watching him set up tables where wealthy Pittsburgh ladies, who were members of the Garden Club, would sell geraniums and English lavender to raise money for the Parks Conservatory.

I enjoyed some freedom in the park where Richard Beatty Mellon's grand estate once stood—the largest mansion in Pittsburgh in its prime. I spent most of my time playing in the beautiful walled garden with its lovely Gothic fountain. I held my fingertips under the cascading water and took in the aroma of the early booms of daffodils and crocus. Dad would let me play alone in this area of the park since he knew I wouldn't stray. I suspect his comfort also came from Mellon Park being his territory. Unlike our gritty Larimer Avenue neighborhood, Dad had some control over the surroundings here.

When Dad occasionally checked on me, I begged him to lift me onto the garden wall where I could stand with his hands firmly around me and take in the grassy hillside sloping down to Fifth Avenue. When his work was finished, Dad and I walked down Shady Avenue to the corner of Fifth, where we caught the streetcar home. Dad let me carry his empty lunch box in one hand while he held my other hand securely in his.

* * *

I stopped by Sean's new duplex one spring afternoon during the pandemic. I looked forward to the outside yard visits with him and Alex, where we could see each other while keeping a safe distance. Sean was kneeling beside Alex's bike, fiddling with the wheels while she stood beside him, arms folded, face determined. Sean appeared to be removing the training wheels, and, ironically, Alex argued to keep them on.

"I might fall without them, Daddy."

"You don't need them," Sean told her. "You're a good rider."

I called hello, Sean looked up from the bike, and Alex came running, arms waving, yelling, "Hi, Nonna!"

"It looks like you're getting the training wheels off," I said.

"No," she replied. "I'm not ready."

I listened while Sean and Alex negotiated, he seemingly wanting her to experience riding without the training wheels, and she resolved in her decision that she wasn't yet ready. More stubborn than her father, Alex flatly refused to ride the bike without extra support. Finally, they reached a compromise, lifting the wheels slightly rather than removing them. It struck me how Sean is a different father than my dad, how he balances giving Alex freedom and protection, allowing her to think for herself, and viewing her as her own person. I watched as Alex mounted the bike and headed up the long concrete walkway that lined the length of their yard. The bike started to lean to one side, and she struggled to keep it upright.

"Ride faster," Sean yelled. "You can do it."

One of my favorite photos of Dad and me.

Riding my bike around
Larimer schoolyard.

IV

Running Numbers for Chocolate

Late one summer afternoon when I was six, I played alone in front of Mr. Corazza's grocery store. I could only venture beyond my block if my mother walked me to Grandma's house or to play with one of my friends on Orphan or Lenora Street. I didn't mind playing in front of our building. It was my place in the neighborhood, where I belonged.

I was on threezies in a game of jacks when Mr. Galiano, one of the neighborhood men, called out to me.

"Linda, come here," he waved.

That's the day it began—my chocolate gig.

Mr. Galiano was a fixture on our block, spending most days with a small group of men sitting on the stoop in front of Mrs. Gentilcore's chicken store a few doors away. He was stocky with a bald head and a round face, made larger by a mass of chewing tobacco tucked in his cheek. In the summer, Mr. Galiano usually wore a straw hat with a black grosgrain band. Neighborhood men and women would stop by to hand him small pieces of paper that he would slip into the hat band.

Three types of men lived in our neighborhood: working men like my dad, shopkeepers like Mr. Corazza, and small-time criminals. Everyone coexisted, sharing the taverns, shops, neighborhood streets, and the church, which seemed to resemble organized crime in some ways—rigidly hierarchical with established guidelines, similar vows of silence, and unquestioned power. In our neighborhood, it was okay to violate the law, but not your family, or the church, or the "wize guys."

Larimer Avenue was my mother's neighborhood. She was born and raised there. While it would be years before anyone in my mom's family became involved in petty crime, she was a neighborhood girl, enculturated from birth into the ways of this place. She understood the roles adopted by each type of neighbor; she recognized where power resided; she knew how things worked, all lessons that I would come to learn as well. When I was a young adult, Mom confided that she had dated an underboss for one of the big five crime families. "We were young at the time," she explained, "before he moved up from soldier to underboss."

It was exciting that a mob boss might have been my father. I could have been a mafia princess, my wrists adorned with diamond bracelets, taking frequent vacations to Rome, maybe driving an Alpha Romeo. Organized crime translated to wealth and freedom from hard work. Of course, Mom had also dated the huckster.

Criminal activity didn't seem unusual in my family. My favorite uncle was a dealer in a private club run by the Italian mob. When I was old enough, he shared with me that he had attended the infamous 1957 Apalachin, New York meeting where he dealt cards for the one hundred or so Mafioso bosses who met there. Uncle told the story with some degree of pride. My mom's oldest sister ran a numbers book out of her small apartment in a public housing high rise. Her oldest son was her numbers boss. For us, small-time crime was part of the norm, an accepted fact of life for the working poor.

On the other hand, my dad was an outsider who moved to Larimer Avenue when he married Mom. He wasn't a neighborhood boy but became acquainted with the guys sitting on the stoop. Dad liked to play the numbers. On the Saturday after pay day, he too would stop in front of the chicken store and drop off his folded piece of paper along with a one-dollar bill.

Dad had a system for selecting which number he'd play. It involved methodically recording which ones hit each day in a little brown vinyl-covered notebook. Dad would study the numbers, the frequency, and the order in which they came out in an attempt to calculate the odds.

This, mind you, without a computer or even a calculator. Dad also consulted a tattered paper "dream book" where he would look up dreams to determine their meaning, not in the Freudian sense, but to correlate the dream to a three-digit number. Dad would thumb through the yellowed pages of the dream book. Dreamed of frying zucchini flowers? Play 638. Dreamed you were sneezing? Play 712 for one sneeze, 529 if you sneezed twice, and play 483 if you sneezed three times. While I overheard conversations between my dad and uncle about playing the numbers—which number to play, whether it was best to play it straight or boxed, and so on—I didn't understand how it all worked or who was involved, and I certainly didn't know that the numbers game was illegal.

I walked toward Mr. Galiano, past the baskets of tomatoes and peaches that lined the front of the grocery and past Henry Grasso's store, where links of plump sausages hung in the window.

As I approached, Mr. Galiano pulled the little pieces of folded paper from his hat band. "Here," he said in a raspy voice, "take these across the street to the candy store, and they'll give you a chocolate bar."

"I'm not allowed to cross the street," I replied.

Mr. Galiano and his friends howled with laughter. "Come on. I'll cross you."

It was a peculiar request, but the chocolate bar piqued my interest, and the storefront had always appeared empty, so I was curious to see the inside.

I stuffed my jacks in one pocket of my shorts and the tiny pink rubber ball in the other. Mr. Galliano placed the folded papers in my hand and closed my fingers carefully around them. Then, he walked me to the curb and looked each way.

"All clear," he said. "Go ahead and cross."

Larimer Avenue was the commercial center of our neighborhood, busy with cars and shoppers and lined with stores selling groceries, hardware, and household goods, Conte's drug store, Ursula's beer store, and a gas station on the corner by the Larimer Bridge. I had never been on the other side of Larimer Avenue without my mother. We always crossed together, whether we were on our way to my grandmother's house two blocks away or when we went to Ursula's beer store across from our apartment to say hello to my mother's long-time friend. Now, I was crossing the street by myself, and I knew my mother wouldn't approve.

I ran across the street and onto the pavement. As I reached for the door handle of the candy store, I noticed grime on the door and the glass storefront windows. I left the sunlit street outside and entered the dimly lit store. The large room seemed strangely empty, with only one candy case—also with dirty glass—in the center. I studied the options in the case: Clark Bar, Baby Ruth, Oh Henry. My favorite, Mounds Bar, was nowhere in sight. Nothing compared to the rich dark chocolate and coconut filling of a Mounds Bar. As I stared at the disappointing selection, someone approached through a door in the back of the store.

"Well, young lady, what brings you here?"

I looked up at a tall man with thick dark hair and a greying mustache. Immaculately dressed in a crisp white shirt, it occurred to me that he was the only thing in the store that was clean. I felt intimidated by his presence. He was someone I didn't know, a stranger to me in my neighborhood. His dress, neatly trimmed mustache, and the way he carried himself with poise told me he wasn't one of the guys from the stoop.

"I have pieces of paper," I stammered, "and Mr. Galiano said I could get a chocolate bar."

The man threw his head back, laughing. "Well, come with me," he said, opening the door to reveal a back room. "You don't want that stale candy. I have some in the back."

The cramped back room held a desk littered with papers and a few men sitting around on wooden chairs.

"We have a delivery," said the dark-haired man smiling as he took the folded papers from my hands.

I watched as he passed them to a portly man with thinning hair and glasses sprawled in a chair behind the desk. Then he reached on a shelf and pulled down several boxes containing chocolate bars. As soon as I saw the dark brown carton with the familiar lettering, I knew I hit pay dirt.

Each afternoon, I'd walk to the chicken store and Mr. Galiano would hand me the small papers from his hat band and watch while I crossed the street. I'd deliver them to the tall man with the mustache in return for a Mounds Bar. It was perfection.

I had delivered the papers in exchange for chocolate bars for several days when I climbed the steps to our second-floor apartment late one afternoon in time for dinner. As I walked in the door, I smelled the aroma of home-fried potatoes. My mom turned from the stove when she heard me come in.

"I've been waiting for you." Then, she looked at me closely. "Where did you get chocolate?" I realized that I must not have wiped my mouth. I didn't respond, and she asked again. "Linda, where did you get chocolate?"

Even at six years old, I knew not to test my mother. So, I told her the whole story.

Her face stiffened. "Get cleaned up for dinner," she said quietly.

I had no sooner washed my face and hands at the kitchen sink when my dad came in. Dad worked as a laborer for the City of Pittsburgh's parks department. He left each morning, lunch pail in hand, and took the streetcar to Mellon Park in Shadyside. After a day of tending to park trails, trimming hedges, and maintaining equipment, Dad returned tired and hungry. His arrival meant it was time for dinner, and we sat at the kitchen table within minutes.

I'm not sure what motivated my mom to tell Dad about the chocolate. "Guess what Linda did today?" Out poured every detail.

Dad put down his fork, straightened in his chair, and stared at me. His hazel eyes met mine, and his face lacked expression. I couldn't tell what he was thinking.

My dad was over six feet tall with muscular arms and broad shoulders, yet he generally spoke softly and sparingly, even when angry. Once, some years later, when my little sister fell and hit her head on the corner of a marble-topped coffee table, my dad, silent and calm, picked up the table right there in the living room and methodically broke off each leg one at a time while my mother watched in horror. She loved that table. But Dad repeatedly warned that a marble top with sharp edges was unsafe with a toddler around.

I had never been on the wrong end of my father's anger, so I braced myself for what might come. I wasn't afraid of him; Dad had never raised his hand or voice to me, but I was worried that I might have somehow disappointed him. He got up from his chair, went to the door, and left the apartment without a word.

My mom went after him. "Just let it be," she cried out. "It won't happen again. Dan, please!"

I had no idea where my dad was going or why Mom was so upset. I felt a bit uneasy that my eating chocolate before dinner had caused such an upheaval. Mom returned to the kitchen alone, and she and I sat at the table without eating or talking. We waited. Mom fidgeted in her chair, repeatedly glancing over her shoulder toward the door. I sat still, staring at Mom.

After what seemed like hours (but was likely minutes), Dad walked through the door. He sat in his chair, picked up his fork, took a few bites of cold potatoes, then turned to me. "It's over," he said, and I knew he meant my chocolate gig.

We never spoke of it again.

After that day, Mr. Galiano didn't call to me. He avoided even looking at me when I played on the sidewalk near the chicken store. Sometimes, I'd see him leave the stoop and walk across the street. I envied him and wondered if he would get a candy bar.

My brief stint running numbers caused me to make some observations about my neighborhood. I noticed that the men who sat on the stoop and sometimes stood on the sidewalk in front of the candy store disappeared inside when a police car drove down Larimer Avenue. I wondered what they might have to hide. I also noticed a distinction between the working men who left home early each morning on a streetcar and those who didn't seem to ever go to work. The image that has endured is one of my dad, early each morning, lacing up his work boots, kissing my mom and me goodbye, reaching for his black metal lunch pail, then walking down the steps from our apartment and up Larimer Avenue.

V

Baw Baw and the Saint Rocco Festival

My great-grandfather wore his usual white long-sleeved shirt and covered his head with the familiar straw hat despite the August heat. He drained his glass and wiped his handlebar mustache with the back of his hand as he slowly climbed the steps to the bandstand, holding on to the railing to steady himself. This was the moment I had waited for all week when Baw Baw would sing for the crowd at our neighborhood's annual Saint Rocco Festival.

Saint Rocco, the patron saint of cholera and plague victims, surgeons, and dogs, was known for giving all his worldly possessions to the poor and tending to the sick, curing victims of the plague by making the sign of the cross on their foreheads. While he was born in France, he spent part of his life traveling through Italy, performing what the faithful believed to be miracles, and the Italians adopted him as their own. Southern Italian immigrants, in particular, carried their adulation of Saint Rocco and the tradition of his feast day from the old country, clinging to ties with their home *paese* and each other.

Saint Rocco's feast day commenced on Sunday morning with a Mass offered by Father Angelo, the Italian-speaking priest at Our Lady Help of Christians. At the beginning of Mass, the Holy Name Society men wheeled the float with the statue of the saint from behind the sacristy, placing it at the front of the church before the altar, where it stood watching over parishioners. Saint Rocco, a little brown and white plaster dog at his feet, held his staff with one hand and peeled back his brown robe to expose his leg wound with the other. As they approached for communion, the faithful venerated the statue by kissing Saint Rocco's foot, an altar boy standing by with a white cloth to wipe it after each disciple.

After Mass, the Holy Name men glided the float up the church aisle through the huge wooden doors and carried Saint Rocco down the steps to the street. Nick Isaush assembled his musicians on the church steps while Father Angelo and two altar boys took their places in front of the float. Girls in their white communion dresses positioned themselves behind the float, and Nick's band followed—trumpets first, then trombones, and finally, the large bass drum, the big tuba, and crashing cymbals. It was an amazing display.

The procession moved up Meadow Street past Febbraro's Funeral Home and turned right onto Larimer Avenue. At home, Mom and I waited. We didn't attend the special Mass but went to church earlier to be home on time to view the procession. Dad and Uncle weren't much interested and stayed inside reading the Sunday paper, but Mom, Mim, and I were excited to see the spectacle. Mom stuffed a dollar bill in the pocket of her house dress while I ran ahead down the hall. We arrived at Mim's door, and Mom poked her head into the kitchen.

"It's almost time, Olympia."

The three of us headed down the steps and out the front door. Larimer Avenue was packed with neighbors, old men and women waiting to adulate Saint Rocco's statue, kids on bikes, and dogs running into the street. Mr. Corazza and his daughters stood beside us in front of our building. Mrs. Ciorra, Mrs. Faciano, and the other housewives positioned themselves along the curb, chatting with each other. We had waited only a few minutes when I heard it.

"I can hear the band. It's coming!"

"Wait here with me," Mom said, holding my hand tightly as we stood on the sidewalk.

When the procession reached the front of our building, we inched our way into the street. Kids and dogs parted like the Red Sea as the float approached our corner and stopped. I glanced at the statue of

Saint Rocco, then turned my attention to the girls in white First Holy Communion dresses, picturing myself in something similar next spring. As we got closer to the float, I could see the dollar bills the Italian immigrants had pinned to Saint Rocco's sash as an offering for the church. While most likely couldn't afford the donation, the tradition of giving was culturally ingrained in the same way they attended Mass, venerated the statue, and took communion. Mom walked up to the float, made the sign of the cross, and lifted me high enough to pin the dollar on his sash. I felt important, or at least that I was doing something important.

Later in the evening, the religious feast turned into a festival, and Larimer School playground, what we affectionately called "the club yard," bustled with activity. Food stands sold sausage and pepper sandwiches on crusty bread, homemade cannoli, and authentic Italian pizza like the kind that Mim made with a thin crust baked in a rectangle pan. Boys maneuvered their bicycles through the crowd, balloons clothespinned to the wheel spokes so their bikes sounded like noisy lawnmowers. Neighborhood men, most of whom were Baw Baw's friends, drank wine and crowded around a table covered with a red and white checkered plastic tablecloth. Mom and Mim called out to friends as we made our way toward the pizza stand, where I selected a corner piece with lots of cheese.

The bandstand stood at the center of the club yard where Nick conducted his group of musicians. I grasped my mother's hand with one hand and held my pizza with the other as we stood with Mim in front, listening to Italian songs streaming from the stage: "Torna Sorrento," "Santa Lucia," and the upbeat "Tarantella."

A group of men and women made a semi-circle around Mrs. Martinelli, who danced the tarantella with her friend, Mrs. Faciana, everyone clapping and laughing. Mom and Mim liked listening to music and visiting with neighbors at the festival, but my thoughts all day were in anticipation of Baw Baw singing.

I had a special relationship with my great-grandfather, Urbano. Of the thirty or so cousins, I was closest to him. Early on Sunday afternoons, Baw Baw would come to our apartment to collect me. He'd wear his dark-colored baggy pants and blue cardigan sweater, straw hat perched on his head. I liked to wear my favorite green sweater, the one with the Happy Badge I was awarded at school for having no cavities. Baw Baw and I would walk together hand and hand along Larimer Avenue. We'd pass Henry Grasso's sausage store, Larimer School, and Allen's 5 & 10. Our destination was the Islay's ice cream store at the upper end of the street, where Baw Baw would buy me a large cone I'd eat on the way home. We'd walk slowly, my hand securely in his, not speaking but basking in the knowledge that Baw Baw chose to spend time strolling through the neighborhood with me. When we returned to my parents' apartment, he would give me a nickel, my weekly allowance.

Later in the day, I'd see Baw Baw again at Grandma's house, where many of my aunts, uncles, and cousins spent Sundays. He would call to us children as we played. "*Vieni qui; abbracciami,*" asking for us to come and hug him. Most of my girl cousins screamed and ran. Even my cousin Danielle, a year older and much taller than me, took off as fast as her long limbs would carry her. Her younger sister, Jackie, would walk through the small alleyway beside Grandma's house to reach the front porch so she didn't have to go through the kitchen where Baw Baw sat. Maybe they feared his gruff manner and bristly handlebar mustache that looked like someone had glued pieces of straw from grandma's broom over his upper lip. But I was happy to oblige, running into his arms to hug and kiss him. "Leenda," he would say in his thick Italian accent, "You the besta one." His voice was raspy, and his tone brusque. He smelled of cigars and wine. His hands were rough and calloused. I adored him.

Now it was time to hear Baw Baw sing. He staggered to the center of the stage. Nick's band played the first familiar notes of the song, "O Solo Mio," and Baw Baw clutched at the microphone.

"Time to go," my mother said. She turned and walked quickly away from the bandstand, Mim following. Mom gripped my hand tightly, and Mim grabbed my other arm at the wrist so I didn't drop my pizza.

"No, please," I wailed. "I want to hear Baw Baw sing!"

"Maybe we can stay," Mim suggested.

"It's late," Mom insisted. She and Mim picked up their pace as they weaved through the food stands toward the opening in the club yard fence, and my six-year-old legs had to break into a jog to keep up.

"Why can't I stay and hear Baw Baw? He'll be looking for me!"

My mother and Mim glanced at each other.

I spent a lifetime learning how much my mother cared about appearances. Mom seemed to respect traditions like observing the Saint Rocco procession, pinning money on the statue, and attending the festival. Yet, I suspect that what she may have valued more was the appearance of keeping tradition, friends watching her stand on the curb waiting for the procession, and neighbors seeing her lift her child to pin a dollar on Saint Rocco's sash. She seemed to find little value in Baw Baw standing center stage singing "O Solo Mio." Instead, in her mind, his public intoxication sullied her reputation. It still pains me to see Baw Baw relegated to something shameful that Mom couldn't accept.

I remember Baw Baw's strong baritone voice, how he sometimes sang while working in Grandma's garden, and how the neighbors smiled hearing him. I wonder if Mom recognized the affection others had for him or if she grasped the significance of his place as the first in our family to immigrate to America, or if she understood the importance that he held for me. How I wish she could have seen him through my eyes, seen my immense love for him.

Years later, I learned of my great-grandfather's drinking. Mom related embarrassing incidents when she and her boyfriend (later to be my father) were sent to retrieve Urbano from the Italian Brotherhood Beneficial Association. He had been ejected from the tavern most nights.

"He was a happy drunk," Mom explained, "but he would drink so much wine that he would sometimes put the waitress' tips in their blouses, and he would insist on singing at the top of his lungs."

I don't know if Mom held love or affection for him. Either way, Baw Baw had caused her much public humiliation. She'd had enough.

Yet, that night, with Nick's band playing in the background and Baw Baw's voice reverberating over the speakers, I couldn't fathom why we were leaving.

"I'll take you to see him at Grandma's tomorrow," Mom said to soothe me. "He'll understand it was late and you couldn't stay." My mom's pace quickened, and I felt my pizza slip from my hand and fall to the ground.

Baw Baw and me on one of our Sunday walks.

VI

My Other Mother

"Which song do you want to sing next?" I asked Alex over my shoulder.

"You pick, Nonna," she replied from her car seat.

I had been singing to Alex since she was born, and she began singing along as soon as she could form words. We especially enjoyed singing songs while we rode in the car.

"How about 'Playmate'? It was one of your daddy's favorites."

"Did you teach him the same songs you teach me?"

"Yes, baby girl. All the same songs."

"Who taught you, Nonna?"

"Mim."

"Was she your mother?"

I hesitated for a moment, searching for the right words. "She was my other mother." Even as I said it, I knew the phrase was an oversimplification that Alex might understand, but that didn't do justice to my relationship with Mim.

Mim, a nickname my cousin Bobby gave Olympia when we were little, was more than a second mother. Throughout my life, she held a central presence, both a pillar and a comfort. Mim taught me what Mom couldn't, understood what Mom didn't, and forgave what Mom wouldn't. We loved each other without condition.

Mim met my Uncle Felix the night I was born, and two months to the day later, they were married and moved into the building where we lived. Our two apartments took up the entire second floor, and I considered Mim and Uncle's place an extension of my own. I often ate at their kitchen table, played on their back porch, and napped on their couch. We shared the hall bathroom halfway between the two apartments, where Mim sometimes gave me my evening bath. There, soaking in warm bubbles while Mim sat on the side of the tub, she taught me the songs I would teach to my sons and now sing to Alex years later. "Playmate," "I Wanna Be in Chicago Town," and "Barefoot Days." Mim's voice was rich and clear, hitting all the notes. I can still hear my small voice blending with hers:

Barefoot days, when you and I were kids
Barefoot days, the things we always did

My mom didn't teach me songs, and I don't remember her ever singing. Thinking back, it seems a sad revelation. Singing echoed throughout my family. Baw Baw's deep voice singing Italian folk songs in Grandma's backyard, Dad and I crooning along with Perry Como records, and Mim's vocals as much a part of each day as her conversations. Sad that Mom didn't share the joy of song. Her daily life seemed more utilitarian than joyful. Mom taught me how to tie my shoes and set the dinner table. Mim taught me how to embroider colorful flowers at the end of a pillowcase. Mom instructed me how to make my bed and say my prayers. Mim showed me how to dance the jitterbug. Mom trained me to be responsible, while Mim taught me how to have fun.

It seemed they'd always been that way—Mom practical and grounded, Mim free-spirited. Mom and Mim were the closest in age of six girls. The four youngest sisters, Gilda, Mim, Mom, and Dahlia, shared the tight confines and crowded sleeping arrangement of two beds in a third-floor bedroom growing up. Their father would call them from the bottom of the steps at bedtime, and each girl would respond, "Goodnight, Papa." Mom told me how many nights she answered for herself and

Mim, covering for her adventurous sister, who liked to stay out late. Things didn't seem to change much as the two sisters got older.

Mim liked to gamble, and she and her good friend, Mrs. Gentilcore, who lived a few doors away, regularly joined some of the other neighborhood women to play cards—mostly poker, sometimes gin rummy. They also frequented Bingo games with Mrs. Ciorra, our next-door neighbor, and faithfully hit every church Bingo in the vicinity of Larimer Avenue. Mim was lucky and won often.

When I was old enough to read the numbers and suits, I learned to gamble and joined Mim and Uncle playing cards. Mim provided stacks of pennies from her cookie jar so that we could place bets. She taught me poker variations like "Jacks to open, trips to win," or "Follow the queen." I quickly learned that three of a kind beat two pair, a straight beat three of a kind, a flush beat a straight, and so on. I felt grown up playing cards with Mim and Uncle.

One recent Saturday afternoon, Alex and I were sprawled on my office floor, deep into playing a game of UNO, when Sean arrived to collect her.

"I'm not ready to go yet, Daddy," Alex said. "Nonna and I are playing the tying game, and we have to finish."

Sean plopped in the easy chair in front of the window, watching Alex and I throw down cards—a series of blue, then green. We were down to just one card each when I drew a wild card.

"Red," I declared, throwing down the card.

Alex grinned and discarded a red nine. Then she leapt to her feet, arms in the air, and sang, "I dream of Jeannie with the light brown hair."

"Oh my God, it's Mim!" Sean howled with laughter.

For reasons unknown, Mim had a habit of singing this old Stephen Foster song whenever she won a hand at cards. It got so that as soon as she uttered the first notes, everyone else groaned and folded their cards. I thought Mim's ritual entertaining and charming. I taught Alex the song's first line, and she adopted the routine, singing enthusiastically each time she won a hand. I also taught her Mim's practice of announcing, "This isn't a hand; it's a foot," whenever she was dealt a bad hand. I loved watching Alex mimic Mim, remembering her this way.

I'm intentional about passing along to my granddaughter some of what I learned from Mim. She taught me how to do the hokey pokey and to make pizzelle cookies holding a heavy cast iron pizzelle maker over the stove, saying a Hail Mary on each side to time it perfectly. Mim also taught me how to be open, playful, loving.

When I was about five, Mim got a little black-and-white dog. I don't know his breed; he was probably a mutt. She and Uncle handpicked him from various dogs in the stacked cages at the Humane Society on Hamilton Avenue. He was about twelve or fifteen pounds and mostly white, with a few black spots on his body and around his eyes. One ear was white, and the other black and they were in a perpetual state of perked up. Mim named him Rudy.

Rudy became a sibling to me. We played ball on the concrete side porch common to our two apartments, and we chased each other up and down the hallway, Rudy barking and me squealing until either Mom or Mim put a stop to it. Rudy was a welcome addition to my second-floor extended family, especially since my mother wouldn't allow me to have a pet. The only exception she made was the small yellow canary she bought when I turned five. I called him Happy since he always sang, but I thought he was a senseless pet because I couldn't really play with him. Mom wouldn't let me take Happy out of his cage.

Mim seemed better suited to be a pet mom, and she treated Rudy like her child. She cooked meals of ground beef and gravy and let him sit on a chair to eat at a small wooden table on her back porch. She even made clothes for Rudy, like the little blue coat she crocheted for him to wear outside when fall turned into winter. Mim had always made my Halloween costumes and started making them for Rudy. One year he wore a little red jacket and cap that made him look like a canine jockey, and another year he was dressed in a blue policeman's outfit complete with badge and hat. I wore a cowgirl costume that Halloween with a skirt and blouse Mim decorated with fringe and a hat with a string tie under my chin. Mim took Rudy out onto Larimer Avenue on his leash for the neighbors to see, but he didn't join me trick or treating up and down the block.

The summer I was six, Mim decided to have a first birthday party for Rudy. She hung colored paper streamers on her back porch and bought party hats for herself, Rudy, and me. She let me help to make a birthday cake: vanilla with chocolate icing. I preferred a chocolate cake, but Mim said vanilla was better for dogs. We decorated the cake with blue and yellow flowers and "Happy Birthday Rudy" on the top. Then the three of us donned our party hats and took our places at the small table on the back porch. Uncle came out with his Polaroid camera to take a photo of the comical site: the pigtailed little girl, the frisky pup wearing an absurd party hat, and Mim looking sophisticated despite it all. She lit the candles, and we sang to Rudy, then she served us each a piece of cake. Rudy got the most generous portion and gobbled it quickly, his little black and white ears bobbing up and down over his plate like a cork in a bucket of water.

Mim and I were eating the last bites of cake when Rudy leapt from his chair, rotated in small circles with his nose to the ground, and then started to choke. As he circled the back porch, Rudy gagged and heaved, vomiting multiple puddles of vanilla birthday cake. Mim jumped from her seat and rushed into the kitchen to fetch Rudy some water. Rudy followed her inside, continuing to retch cake and chocolate icing. I followed Rudy, shrieking.

Mom must have heard the commotion. She ran down the hall and into Mim's kitchen to find Rudy continuing to heave and Mim in a frenzy chasing him around the room with a bowl of water. Mom took one look at the dog vomit on Mim's clean kitchen floor, turned to me, and said, "See? This is why I don't let Happy out of his cage."

Mim didn't seem concerned about her kitchen floor. With Uncle's help, she finally caught Rudy, nuzzled him in her arms, and wiped his mouth with her clean tea towel while repeating, "It's okay, Rudy. You're okay."

When I was nine, we had all left Larimer Avenue. Mim and Uncle bought a car, and they took me along to visit Uncle's sister and her family in the Oakland section of Pittsburgh, where Agnes and her husband, Ken, ran a Chinese restaurant. The Bamboo Garden sat on the corner of Meyran and Forbes Avenue, the main street in Oakland, and was a bustling family business. Born in China, Ken was the cook, and Agnes served as hostess. They hired a Mexican immigrant named Maxine to wash dishes, and she became part of the family. Ken and Agnes' sons were about my age, and we often hung out in the restaurant eating huge bowls of chicken fried rice and opening piles of fortune cookies until Maxine would catch us and yell in her thick Mexican accent, "Don't do that! They for the peoples! No for you!"

I loved the Bamboo Garden. It was filled with the smells of spices, peanut oil, and sautéed vegetables. Sitting in the family booth next to the double swinging doors that led to the kitchen, I could hear the loud banter of Ken and Maxine and the blend of their Chinese and Mexican accents. The restaurant matched the diverse flavor of the Oakland neighborhood. It wasn't just the international food but an exotic feel to the whole place that carried me far from my mother's restraint and concern for conformity. It had an authentic exuberance about it that I attributed to Mim and Uncle, and I wanted nothing more than to embody their energy, feel comfortable in their skin, and be more like Mim.

Forbes Field, the home of the Pittsburgh Pirates, was also located in Oakland. I only remember attending two baseball games as a child—the first when I was little, and Ursula took my mom and me, and the second time a few years later with Mim and Uncle. But in 1960, when I was thirteen, the Pirates won the World Series, and Mim and Uncle took me to Oakland for the victory parade. The streets were filled with people of all ages, social classes, colors, and nationalities, out to celebrate their beloved Bucs. Benny Benack and his Dixieland band, local musicians made famous by their rendition of "Beat 'em Bucs," were set up at the corner of Forbes and Bouquet Street near the Bamboo Garden. Mim, Uncle, and I sang along with the crowd, clapping our hands and grinning like the rest of the crazed fans.

When the parade started, Benack's band led a stream of late-model convertibles moving slowly down Forbes Avenue. Two of the Pirates sat high on the back of each car, leaning out the sides to shake hands with the crowd. My eyes were peeled for Roberto Clemente, the Pirate's star right fielder and my favorite player. When I spotted him, I was relieved to see him sitting on the side of the car closest to my side of the street. The crowd started cheering, "Arriba!" Clemente's nickname. I let go of Uncle's hand and ran, arm outstretched, towards the red convertible. Clemente looked down at me, smiled, and reached out his hand to shake mine. The moment passed, and the car moved on. I turned back to Mim and Uncle, who were congratulating me and screaming, "Arriba!"

When I got home that night, I told my mom about the parade and how we sang and yelled. I told her about shaking Clemente's hand and how Mim and Uncle were so excited for me.

"You still have to wash your hands before you go to bed," she said. Mom was nothing if not true to form. I lied and said that I would.

As I got older, I sometimes wondered why Mim and Uncle never had children. They were devoted second parents, playful, caring, and clearly taking joy in sharing my life. My question was answered late on New Year's Eve when I was about fifteen, and Mim and Uncle were celebrating with my mom and dad at our apartment. While my parents didn't drink, Mim and Uncle were clinking the ice in their glasses of whiskey and ginger ale. As we approached midnight, Mim's usual cheerful mood turned morose. She was crying, something I'd never seen before, and Mom took her into the kitchen for a glass of water and some consolation. Standing in the hallway, I overheard Mim tell my mom, "Felix found out about my botched abortion. He knows why I could never have a baby."

I was stunned. I knew what an abortion was, but I didn't grasp then the danger of illegal back-alley abortions when they were sordid and hard to find, when women were rendered infertile or dead. My shock turned to anguish for Mim and Uncle and then for me. I realized I was the substitute for the child they could never have.

Thinking back, I suspect Mom and Mim each longed for some aspect of the other's life. Mom must have looked with envy at Mim, adventurous and seemingly unconcerned with outward appearances. Mim laughed out loud in public, wore pencil skirts with stiletto heels, and seemed almost weightless, like a helium balloon rising above my grounded mother. And yet, I'm sure that Mim wanted what Mom had: children to tuck in at night, wake for school, and care for when they're sick. Children who called her "Mom."

* * *

Alex and I were playing our game, where we took turns teaching each other dance steps. I'd already taught her the twist, and she shared a little dance she had learned in kindergarten. When it was my turn again, I reached down to help place her bare feet in the five ballet positions. She struggled with fourth and fifth but insisted she wanted to learn how to be a ballerina. Then it was her turn, and she started into a dance that she'd created, leaping up and down the hallway, knees high, arms flung in the air. I followed, mimicking her steps, and she squealed with laughter. We flopped onto the sofa cushions, and I hugged Alex close, telling her in English and Italian, "I love you, baby girl, *ti amo*," to which she replied, "*Ti amo molto*, Nonna." Loving comes easily to us, and I'm grateful for this gift from Mim.

Rudy's birthday party.

VII

Bless Me, Father, for I Have Sinned

I knelt in the pew next to Jason, my younger son, while the priest held up the chalice of wine. The altar boy rang the bells three times, and Jason and I tapped our fists against our hearts with each chime. This was the familiar ritual that I had carried with me since childhood. The priest came to the front of the altar and stood at the center of the main aisle. Congregants left their pews, one row at a time, walked to the front, and stood before the priest with cupped hands before them. The priest held up the host and pronounced, "The body of Christ," to which the parishioner replied, "Amen."

Jason and I had attended Sunday Mass together since he entered Central Catholic High School the previous year. I'd discovered he wasn't always truthful about homework and sometimes about his comings and goings. "You need confession," I told him. Like my older son, Sean, Jason had been baptized in the Catholic Church, but I gave up on the practice of Catholicism when they were little. At this point, however, I thought the sacrament of confession might be just what this kid needed to be accountable. Yet, I wonder now if it was truly accountability that I wanted to teach him. Or was it the perpetuation of guilt handed down through the generations, like my grandmother's recipe for pasta sauce.

Surprisingly, Jason didn't put up much of an argument, and he made his First Confession and First Holy Communion. To support him, we started attending Mass together. Yet, I didn't always walk up to the front of the church with Jason to receive communion. It depended on my mood. Divorced and remarried, I was not permitted by church law to receive communion, my punishment for the sin of escaping a terrible marriage. The sacrament was no longer important to me, but some days I resented being told what I could or couldn't do. On those days, I marched to the front of the church, palms open in front of me, proclaiming a loud "Amen" as I stared into the eyes of an unsuspecting priest. *There*, I thought. Later, I would usually feel guilty. I never told my mother that I took communion, and I'd promise myself that I wouldn't do it again. Until the next time.

Growing up, Catholicism was a mixed bag in my house. Dad didn't talk much about religion or the church. I never saw him pray, and I don't recall him ever asking me if I said my prayers. He stayed home on Sunday mornings reading the paper while Mom and I attended Mass. His detachment might be attributed to the fact that he lost his mother at age two. Perhaps without a mom to instill religious observance, Dad never developed the habit or the interest.

My mom was a prayerful woman who regularly petitioned the saints for intervention. She appealed to Saint Anthony to help find lost items. She prayed to Saint Francis of Assisi since the priests at our church were Franciscan, and I suspect that Mom thought that gave her an inside track. Most often, though, she prayed to the Blessed Mother. A rosary hung from the headboard on her side of the bed, and a two-foot-high plaster statue of the Blessed Virgin sat on her chest of drawers. Mary had alabaster skin and bright blue eyes, the color of her long veil. Her head tilted downward in saintly innocence. I frequently noticed Mom speaking to the statue but couldn't hear what she was saying.

From as early as I can remember, Mom had me kneel at the side of my cot to say bedtime prayers. She taught me the sign of the cross and how to ask God's blessing for our family members. This ritual would take a while with parents, grandmother, great-grandfather, many aunts, uncles, and cousins. We inevitably overlooked some family members, and it would get so late that we were forced to exclude friends and neighbors.

Mom faithfully attended Mass each Sunday wearing her best housedress and shoes and a white lace chapel veil bobby-pinned to the crown of her head that reminded me of the doilies on my grandmother's buffet.

She paraded down the church aisle like a politician, stopping to greet friends and neighbors. "Mrs. Faciana, how are you doing? Hi Angie, how's your mother? Tell her I asked about her." She passed the neighborhood men who usually stood outside the IBBA; they seemed out of place sitting in church pews wearing silk suits. Mom sat near the front, but not in the first few rows occupied by old women dressed in black, rosary beads between gnarled fingers, lips moving silently. When she arrived at the pew where she sat each week, Mom genuflected so that her knee met the cool marble floor before entering the pew. Then she fell to her knees, rested her chin on her folded hands, closed her eyes, and prayed for what seemed like an uncomfortably long time.

One Sunday, when I was a young adult and accompanied Mom to Mass, I noticed that she knelt in prayer for a prolonged time, even for her. I asked her what she prayed for when she finally sat back in the pew. "That woman over there," she said, pointing to a thin, dark-haired woman kneeling in a pew across the aisle. "She's praying so hard, so I asked God to grant whatever she needed."

Starting at age five, Mom took me along to Mass each Sunday. I liked wearing my nicest dress and black patent leather Mary Janes. Mom paid extra attention to my braids and put small ribbons at the end of each instead of the usual rubber bands. While I liked attending church with Mom, Mass was long and dull. The priest mumbled in Latin with his back to the congregation, so I had no idea what was said. I followed Mom standing, kneeling, sitting, and then standing again, and I learned to memorize and repeat the responses. But I didn't much like the smell of the incense or getting damp from the scattering of holy water the priest sprinkled from a container at the end of a long chain. Most parishioners read from the booklets at each pew with songs and readings for every Sunday throughout the Catholic calendar. Some people read the church bulletin. Mostly, I stared at the statues and stained-glass windows. Ironically, I felt even less engaged as a teenager after Vatican II when the priest faced the congregation and spoke English. Something magical was lost.

In the fall of 1953, when I was six, I started catechism classes. Many of my public school classmates came from Catholic families, but like my parents, most couldn't afford parochial school tuition. So, when it was time to study religion, we went to catechism at Our Lady Help of Christians, where we learned Catholic doctrine and liturgy, rites and rituals, and the essentials of preparing for our First Confession and First Holy Communion the following spring.

Classes were taught by Sister Carmelita, one of the Franciscan nuns affiliated with Help of Christians School. She was a petite young woman whose heavy brown robes engulfed her slender frame. She had a broad face, dark bushy eyebrows over penetrating brown eyes, and a thin line in place of a smile. Her movements were rigid, and her voice had a firmness that made clear she was unaccustomed to humor and wouldn't tolerate nonsense. No one tested Sister Carmelita.

We were each given a small green paper-backed book with the words *Baltimore Catechism* on the cover. We learned about God, Jesus, and the saints, many of whom were martyred. We studied the ten commandments and how to recite the prayers in the rosary. Invariably, we said lots of prayers for the poor souls in purgatory—people who, for some inexplicable reason, were forbidden to enter heaven and existed trapped in a "waiting room." Sister said it was important to pray for them.

Mostly, Sister talked about sin. Sins were categorized as either mortal, the big ones, or venial, the small sins. I figured since I was only six, I didn't need to concern myself with mortal sins, so I concentrated on trying to determine what the venial sins were. We learned the Act of Contrition, which we were required to recite for the priest at our First Confession. It ended with, "I firmly resolve, with the help of Thy grace, to sin no more and avoid the near occasion of sin." Back then, I had no idea what it meant to avoid the near occasion of sin. I assumed that it must be important, so this was the cause of some distress.

Our entire catechism teaching seemed centered on fear, guilt, and sin—fear that we would sin and guilt because we knew that we were bound to be sinners. We were also warned that Satan was always around to tempt us, so we had to be on guard. Sister Carmelita explained that we each had a guardian angel who watched over us; I hoped mine would steer me in the right direction. Years later, when I shared my catechism experience with Sean, he remarked, "Why would anyone do that to a child?" Why, indeed.

Catechism classes cemented what became my years-long struggle with guilt. While the church presumably set out to provide guidance, what it actually taught was shame and constant self-reproach. I felt somehow responsible, not only for my shortcomings but for others. Did I do enough to keep my son in school, prevent that student from failing, or keep my dear second husband alive? In the Catholic Church, one is born with original sin, and it goes downhill from there, followed by a persistent focus on blaming oneself for all things within and beyond our control. Catholicism thrives on a negativity that eclipses all else. A Baptist friend explained to me recently what she concluded was the primary distinction between her church and mine. "You all kept Christ on the cross," she said. "We focus on his resurrection."

One recent fall afternoon, Jason and I took a walk through my neighborhood. We stopped on a bench in a little park to extend our visit, and the topic of his Catholic high school education came up. I asked him what he thought about Catholic teaching and, particularly, about confession.

"I never bought what they were selling," he said, "from the talking snake and original sin up to offering extra credit for attending a right to life march."

I remember feeling proud of Jason when he refused to attend the march.

"What about guilt?" I asked, wondering if my son suffered the same affliction as I. "Did the church make you feel guilty? Do you still?"

"Catholic guilt? That's just them putting their stuff on you. Judgment is their thing. If I ever feel guilty, it's because I know I did something wrong, so I fix it. It has nothing to do with religion."

I felt relieved that Jason seemed to have divested himself of any Catholic guilt that I or the church attempted to ingrain in him and replaced it with a healthy sense of personal responsibility.

In the spring, when I was seven, our catechism class prepared to receive the sacraments. Our First Confession, what the church called the Sacrament of Reconciliation, was scheduled a month before our First Holy Communion in May. Sister repeatedly emphasized that we must make a "good" confession. I wondered what that meant and what one does, or fails to do, to make a "bad" confession.

Sister also explained the importance of keeping what was said in the confession box private between the confessor and the priest. "If you're in line and you can hear anyone inside the box talking, just sing a song to yourself," she said.

When the day arrived, we sat pressed side by side in the pews lined up on each side of the ornately carved wooden confessional. The church was stuffy, and I was warm, but at least there was no incense smothering what little fresh air flowed from the open doors at the rear of the church. One by one, my classmates took turns going into one of the small doors on each side of the confessional. Then the rest of us would slide over one spot. Jimmy Scrimma was next to me, and when it was his turn, he went into the small box and banged the door closed. The noise echoed through the quiet church. Jimmy was only in there a few moments when I heard his voice reverberate across the marble floors, filling the church's high ceilings. "Bless me, Father, for I have sinned. This is my First Confession."

I certainly didn't want to hear what sins Jimmy had to confess, especially any mortal ones. I remembered Sister's instructions, so I began singing "Cross Over the Bridge," the Patti Page song that was so popular on the radio that spring with lyrics about reckless living and mending one's ways.

I was singing as loud as I could so the other kids wouldn't hear poor Jimmy when suddenly I felt my hair yanked from behind. Sister Carmelita grabbed one of my braids and dragged me from the pew into the church aisle. My feet hurried to keep up with Sister, who marched quickly toward the back of the church, my braid in her hand and my head and body following. When we got to the church vestibule where Mom and the other mothers waited, Sister released my braid and pulled Mom aside, speaking to her in a hushed yet animated tone. Sister's arms flapped, and her dark eyes flared under her brown nun's habit. She looked like an angry, veiled owl. Mom listened, her eyes wide and shifting back and forth from Sister to me. I stood waiting, wondering what I had done wrong. Mom finally turned to me and calmly asked if I knew any hymns. I said that I didn't. "Then go back to your pew and just hum quietly to yourself while you wait your turn."

Ultimately, I made my First Confession. I remembered the words to the prayers, and I confessed what I felt was a reasonable collection of sins. "I crossed the street without an adult one time, I lied about losing my skate key on the sidewalk when I actually lost it playing in Mrs. Genticore's coal yard, and I talked back to my mother three times." Talking back three times was an estimate, but I imagined God would be okay with my best guess.

After I left the confessional box, I folded my hands at my chest and walked solemnly to a pew near the front of the church. I knelt on the padded kneeler and recited the prayers Father gave me as penance: one Our Father, one Hail Mary, and one Glory Be. Father said I was absolved of my sins, but I didn't feel any different.

In the years that followed, I went to confession regularly. As a teenager, I liked to confess to Father Angelo, who didn't understand much English. Mom was friends with the other priests at our church; she was a member of the Christian Mothers Guild, volunteered at church fundraisers, and even had some of the priests over to our house for dinner occasionally. I was sure they'd recognize my voice in the confessional, so Father Angelo was the safe bet. Yet, the ritual of confession stayed just that: a ritual. I never did feel much different before and then after absolution. My guilt was so ingrained that it almost didn't matter what the priest or God thought. I realized that it was my own forgiveness that I sought, but it remained elusive.

My First Holy Communion was anti-climactic after the ordeal of confession. My parents gave me a little white leatherette-covered prayer book and a rosary with small white beads that I carried to the altar to receive communion. Mim bought me the white lace and tulle communion dress, which was pretty but scratchy, and she sewed my veil and headpiece by hand. At Mass, each child received a prayer card to mark the occasion. Mine had a picture of the Virgin Mary surrounded by bouquets of white flowers and with angelic-looking children gathered at her feet. She looked like the statue on Mom's dresser.

After church, Mom and I returned to our apartment for a lunch that Mim had prepared. Dad and Uncle attempted to make a fuss about my receiving communion, but they seemed more interested in Mim's pasta with broccoli and fried pizza dough. Ursula stopped by and gave me an envelope with a "Congratulations on your First Holy Communion" card. Inside was a crisp five-dollar bill. After lunch, we all walked across the street so Uncle could take a picture of me in front of Ursula's beer store. I squinted into the sun and tried my best to look dignified. When the planned part of the day finally ended, I was glad to change into my shorts and t-shirt. The entire Holy Communion ritual left me somewhat underwhelmed, and I was happy to feel like myself again.

Yet, I do remember feeling some pride at making my communion. It meant that I could accompany Mom during Mass as she walked up the aisle to the front of the church. I belonged to a special club, people who shared that moment of standing before the priest, chalice in hand as he mumbled in Latin, us responding, "Amen," feeling holy. Mom and I were sharing something sacred. We also contributed to a long history of perpetuating a culture of contrition.

The truth is that I never really felt like myself with Catholicism. The practice of it always felt like wearing a holiday dress from a few seasons ago—tight at the waist and damn uncomfortable. Still, I played the dutiful Catholic girl, confessing regularly and attending Mass each Sunday with my mom until I was twenty-one and married, after which I attended alone. I had married a "good Catholic boy" in a church wedding, but he never went to Mass.

At Mom's urging, I volunteered at the church rectory each week on my day off to type the bulletin and run off copies on the mimeograph machine. On one of my volunteering days, I asked the pastor if I could talk with him privately. I needed advice.

I had been married for over ten years at this point with two small sons. It was an awful marriage, and I wanted out. Yet, having been married in the church, I knew divorce would be disgraceful. I felt trapped.

I sat in the leather chair across the desk from the pastor, nervous and clasping my sweaty hands, explaining how my husband drank a lot and was likely an alcoholic. Further, he was physically abusive to me and hit my young sons.

"Father, I need help. I can't stay with this man, and I don't want my sons to grow up in a house with him."

"You were married in the church, correct?"

"Yes, Father. I was."

"Well, you really don't have an option, young lady. You made your bed, and I suggest you find a way to sleep in it."

I didn't go back to the rectory after that day. I stopped going to confession and attending Mass. I didn't want to be part of any religion that would sentence a young family to the horrors of living with an abusive alcoholic. Yet, there were times when I still shared in Catholic rituals. I attended Masses for weddings and funerals, and I sometimes joined my mom at her church because I knew it pleased her. I went to Midnight Mass on Christmas Eve to savor the sound of the massive pipe organ reverberating through the church, see the altar overflowing with red poinsettias, and sit in the pew beside my mother. Like many lapsed Catholics, I participated in religion with the same approach that I went to the gym: occasionally and when it suited me.

I also got a divorce.

It's been years since I've been to confession or Mass. Jason stopped going as well, the one exception being funeral Masses, where he walks to the front of the church for communion and, like his mother, looks into the eyes of an unsuspecting priest and says, "Amen." Thankfully, despite its deep generational roots, Jason seems to have dusted off Catholicism like lint from a sweater.

While I stopped attending Mass, I unfailingly visit churches when traveling. I've taken refuge in the pews of basilicas in Italy, cathedrals in France, and small churches in Charleston. I enjoy studying the statuary and the stained-glass windows, just like when I was a child. I frequently examine the confessionals, sometimes peeking inside, remembering with amusement and discomfort. And I always light a candle. My mom had a custom of lighting candles, usually in front of a statue of the Blessed Mother.

I still keep my old rosary of crystal beads in a silk pouch, and I keep my mother's collection of prayer cards for the dead in the sleeves of a photo album, cards for aunts and uncles long gone, cards for neighbors and friends and distant relatives that I don't remember. I've tried to dispose of these religious artifacts, but throwing them in the trash seems disrespectful, almost sinful. I just can't seem to rid myself of them.

My First Holy Communion photo in front of Ursula's beer store.

VIII

Skipping Church

Pamela was the first to smile at me when I entered my new second-grade classroom. The Larimer School principal and my parents had decided to move me from first to second grade halfway through the year, so I returned from Christmas break to a new teacher and classmates that were a year older and whom I didn't know. Pamela made that first day easier, and we became fast friends.

Pamela had kind brown eyes, a wide smile, and dark braided hair like mine, except that she had a few short braids while I had two long ones. Pamela lived with her mother and older brother in a second-floor apartment over Larimer Pharmacy in the same block as our school. While we were best friends in school and always played together in the schoolyard during recess, we didn't visit each other at home. My friendship with Pamela wasn't the same as with Lucielle Martinelli or Frances Donatelli, whose homes I visited often and whose mothers knew my mother. My friendship with Pamela was somehow different. I didn't question this reality. It just was.

On a Sunday morning in the summer of 1955, when I was eight, I was walking to church alone. My mom wasn't feeling well, so I pleaded with her to let me go to church by myself. After several minutes of begging, she finally agreed.

"Be sure to look both ways when you cross Joseph Street," Mom instructed, "and be especially careful crossing Shetland because it's busier.

And come right home after Mass. Here's the envelope to put in the collection basket, so don't forget it, and—"

"Mom," I interrupted. "I'm eight. I know how to go to church."

I walked up Larimer Avenue heading to Our Lady Help of Christians on Meadow Street, and I was just in front of the school when I saw Pamela walking towards me. Like me, she was dressed in her Sunday clothes—a pretty powder blue dress with a ruffle on the bottom and a pair of black ballet flats. I knew Pamela didn't go to my church, and I assumed she was on her way to one of the Baptist churches nearby.

Pamela and I had played together only a few times over that summer, meeting in the schoolyard on those days when the city employed a teenager to run a day camp for neighborhood kids. We'd draw squares with white chalk on the sidewalk to play hopscotch, and we'd jump rope, singing, "A, my name is Alice, and my husband's name is Al; we come from Alabama, and we sell apples." Then, breathless and sweaty from jumping, we'd sit on the school steps and play board games. The little kids liked Candy Land, but Pamela and I preferred Clue.

Pamela and I waved and called out as we got closer, beaming, delighted to see each other. We stood for a few minutes talking, giggling, and wondering what fourth grade would be like. Then Pamela had an idea.

"Let's skip church," she said.

I felt excited and scared at the same time. I was afraid my mother might find out, but I quickly dismissed my concern in favor of an adventure as Pamela and I considered what we might do.

"We could stay and play here in the school playground," I suggested.

"We'll ruin our church clothes," Pamela said. "Besides, we don't have any games or toys."

We thought a bit more. Then Pamela, who was always resourceful, came up with a plan.

"Let's get a Cherry Coke!"

This sounded like a great idea, and I mentioned that Conte's Drug Store near my house had a soda fountain. Pamela seemed uncomfortable with my suggestion and preferred another soda fountain she knew on Shetland Avenue.

I didn't usually walk down this end of Shetland, but Pamela seemed to know where she was going. We walked a few blocks, passing small brick houses with neatly trimmed front yards, and stopped at a corner drugstore unfamiliar to me. The door was set on an angle at the corner of the building, and a red and white striped canvas awning hung over the doorway. Pamela opened the glass door, and a bell chimed overhead. We went inside and sat at the counter on high swivel stools covered in red vinyl. We were the only customers.

A tall Black man wearing a white jacket stood polishing the counter, and he looked up when we came in. A smile crossed his face, and his eyes had a quizzical look as he approached.

"What have we here?" he asked, seeming amused.

"We'd like two Cherry Cokes, please," Pamela said with confidence.

"Two Cherry Cokes coming up," he replied.

Then Pamela turned to me. "Oh, no. We don't have money!"

I remembered my church envelope and pulled it out of my dress pocket. "I have money," I said proudly, glad that I could contribute to our adventure. I tore open the envelope, and two quarters tumbled out. "Is this enough?" I asked the man behind the counter.

"It's more than enough." He smiled warmly, took just one quarter, and gave me five cents change.

Pamela and I watched as the man scooped ice from a chest just below the counter and emptied it into two glasses. He used a nozzle at the end of a hose to pour Coke into each glass, then pulled a bottle from a shelf behind the counter and carefully poured in a small amount of thick red liquid. He added a straw and gave it a couple of swirls before placing the glasses in front of Pamela and me.

"There you are," he announced.

We took our first mouthfuls of Coke, licked our lips, and laughed as we swirled around high on our stools. We stuck our legs out in front of us, comparing brush burns and bruises, mine from a trip down our back porch steps, Pamela's from a fall when her roller skate came loose. As we examined our legs, I noticed that Pamela's chocolate skin looked pretty against her powder blue dress. We talked and sipped the sweet-tasting Cherry Cokes until we downed the last bit, so our straws made that slurping sound. Then we pushed our glasses away and slid off the stools. We said goodbye to the man behind the counter, and he waved to us as we walked outside into the hot sun.

I thought about how I wanted to continue our Sunday morning fun when Pamela wondered aloud if it was time to go home. We suddenly realized that we didn't know how long to stay away from home. We pondered the question for a while as we slowly strolled back up Shetland toward Larimer Avenue. We thought about walking toward Meadow Street to see if people dressed in church clothes were returning from Mass, but I feared that I might be seen by one of my mother's friends. I suggested we return to the drug store and ask the man behind the counter how long church lasted, but Pamela thought that was silly. We decided to go home and take our chances.

We said our goodbyes and separated, walking in opposite directions on Larimer Avenue. I remember thinking how happy I was that I had run into Pamela. I'd missed seeing her over the summer. I turned around to watch her walk away just as Pamela turned to wave at me. Walking the three blocks to my building, I turned back a few times but lost sight of Pamela as her figure got smaller and finally disappeared.

When I got home and opened the door to our apartment, my mother was in the kitchen, standing in front of the sink.

"How was church?" she asked.

"It was ok," I mumbled without making eye contact.

"Go in and change your clothes, and we'll have lunch."

I went into the bedroom that I shared with my parents. I took off my pink cotton church dress and laid it carefully on my sleeping cot. I knelt on the worn carpet in front of my mother's dresser and opened the bottom drawer where I kept my clothes when an unexplainable sorrow came over me. I sat on the floor in my underwear and cried. I wasn't sure just what brought on the tears. Perhaps I felt guilty over skipping church, lying to my mother, or spending the envelope money on Cherry Cokes. I had betrayed my mother's trust. Or maybe the tears were about Pamela. Perhaps I sensed something about her Blackness and my Whiteness that separated us. Possibly the tears came from an inner place of sadness where I realized that I likely wouldn't see Pamela again that summer.

I looked back on my childhood neighborhood for many years, still believing it was integrated. The Thompsons, who had lived next door, were Black. The Wades, whose backyard met my grandmother's backyard, were Black. Lots of kids in my school were Black. We had played together, noticing the difference in our skin color, some of us trusting that it didn't matter.

I didn't think much of it then, but in hindsight, I realized that Pamela understood that our neighborhood was segregated. She knew the drugstore where she would or wouldn't be welcome. She had to know to survive. My own lack of awareness was a sign of my privilege—I didn't need to know.

Late into adulthood, the eventual realization that my beloved Larimer Avenue was segregated disrupted the nostalgic illusion that I had created of good and decent people living together without regard for their color. I wondered if many of the Italian Americans who held a loving place in my heart were likely racist. They weren't awful people, I reasoned to myself, but a product of their time. Like fish swimming in a bowl, getting wet from the cultural racism surrounding them. The truth stung, though, and the image of my old neighborhood became flawed like a crack in one of my mother's porcelain teacups.

The following summer, we moved from Larimer Avenue, and I never saw Pamela again.

PART TWO

Living with Loss

"Come back. Even as a shadow, even as a dream."
—Euripides

IX

Everything Changed

I was nine when we left our three-room apartment on Larimer Avenue and moved across the Meadow Street Bridge. It was a step up from working poor to working class. We found a place in the last block of Collins Avenue, populated mostly by Italian immigrants who lived in three-story houses with wide front porches and small backyards. Mr. and Mrs. Pampena, who owned the house, lived cramped in four rooms with their son and daughter on the first floor. My family lived on the second and third floors. By the time we moved, I had a one-year-old sister, and a year and a half later, another baby girl was added to our family.

The move changed some things. Mim and Uncle, who also left their Larimer apartment, now lived down the street instead of at the other end of the hall. I had a new school, new friends, and new neighbors. I couldn't walk to Grandma's house. Yet, some things stayed the same. I saw Mim every day. Dad still helped with my homework each night, and I still curled up on the sofa with him to watch the *Friday Night Fights*. Then one day, a couple of years after we moved, everything changed.

It was early morning. The overhead light in my parents' bedroom glowed, and the curtains were pulled back from the front windows, casting the room in bright light. I watched Dr. Angelo Runco examine the small baby as she lay on her blanket atop the white chenille bedspread on my parents' bed. She was wailing and thrusting her tiny legs in the air. My mother stood behind the young doctor, guarding over his shoulder, her deep-set dark eyes fixated on her baby. It was seven o'clock on a chilly fall morning, and I stood in my bare feet and pajamas in the hallway, watching.

The night before, I had listened from my third-floor bedroom to screams erupting from my ten-month-old baby sister, Tisha. I heard my mother's footsteps back and forth on the vinyl tile of the second-floor hall below. I mentally traced her path from her bedroom, past the living room, into the kitchen, and back again. By 6:30 that morning, my exhausted and worried mother called the pediatrician. My dad left early for his job as a laborer since missing a day's wages was not an option. Mom had to deal with the doctor and sick infant alone.

Dr. Runco said that the baby needed to go to the hospital. My mother moved with purpose, her face controlled and seemingly without emotion. She went to the black rotary phone on an end table in the living room and called Mim. "Olympia, I need you to come over right away. I'm taking the baby to the hospital." Then, I watched Mom lift the crying infant, wrap her in the small blanket, then in a larger blanket, and clutching her tightly to her chest, make her way down the steps from our apartment. "Mim's on her way," she said over her shoulder.

Despite the October chill, Mom didn't bother to put a sweater on over her cotton housedress. I followed her down the steps and peered out the front entry window while Dr. Runco helped my mom and baby sister into the back seat of his dark blue sedan and then pulled away. I wondered how long it would be until Mim arrived. At eleven years old, I had never been home without an adult.

Mindful that my three-year-old sister was still asleep in her room, I was relieved when Mim appeared minutes later. I wasn't sure why, but Mim told me to stay home from school that day. She went into my sister's room, woke her, and took us both into the kitchen for breakfast. I could still smell the leftover coffee my dad had poured into his thermos. Mim made herself a cup. The three of us sat at the yellow Formica-topped table, and my sister and I ate Sugar Frosted Flakes with milk while Mim drank coffee. The cold milk tasted fresh on my tongue, and I realized that I hadn't yet brushed my teeth, something I always did when I first woke up. My sister put her hands in her cereal bowl and scooped out frosted flakes, dripping milk down the front of her pajama top. Mim seemed preoccupied, and we didn't talk much. Nothing felt normal.

After breakfast, I spent the morning alone in my room playing records on the small portable turntable that Mim and Uncle bought me for my birthday earlier that year—the Everly Brothers, Elvis, and my new favorite, Frankie Avalon. My room was spacious, taking up the front half of the third floor. The ceilings slanted like the attics of most of the homes on our street, and blue and white wallpaper with small flowers decorated the bottom half of each wall. The floor had a patterned linoleum. It wasn't beautiful, but it was mine—my own space where I crawled under my comforter at night, where I read a copy of *The Yearling* that I borrowed from my school library, where I sat on the wide windowsill listening to my transistor radio, staring at the top branches of the small maple tree in the front yard.

From downstairs, I heard the shrill sound of the phone that seemed to ring every few minutes. Curious, I crept to the bottom of the third-floor steps to hear Mim's end of the conversation. "Norma will be there all day . . . no, I haven't heard anything new . . . don't worry, I'll keep you posted." Several times I heard her repeat the words "tumor" and "heartbreaking." Seeking any sense of normal, I returned to my room as Frankie Avalon crooned "Hey Venus" from my record player.

By afternoon, the day had warmed up, and Mim and I sat on the front porch while my sister napped. Front porches on our street were like village *piazzas* where neighbors congregated to exchange bottles of homemade wine, tomatoes picked from backyard gardens, and neighborhood gossip. Soon after we settled into the glider on our side of the porch, a stream of women came by to check in with Mim. "That poor baby," said one. "Poor Norma," said another.

When Mim went inside to prepare dinner, I stayed on the porch, anxious for my father to come home from work. I kept watch for him, looking over the porch railing and down the hill of our street. When I finally saw my dad walking up Collins Avenue, lunch pail in hand, I hurried to the porch steps to greet him. I felt Dad's hand touch the crown of my head tenderly as he passed. "Wait here, babe," he said. Then he went through the door and up the steps to the second floor. He didn't ask about my day.

We ate dinner that night without Mom, which seemed the most unusual part of that completely strange day. After dinner, Mim bathed my sister and put her to bed. Then Dad, Mim, and I sat in the living room. *Wagon Train* was on the television, but even Ward Bond, the show's star, couldn't hold Dad's interest; he sat staring out the living room window into the dark. Mim, having failed at attempts to start a conversation, sat on the sofa looking into her lap. I found a deck of cards and sprawled on the carpeted floor to play solitaire. We waited for Mom. She returned home later that evening in a taxi. It was the first time I saw anyone in my family ride in a taxi. That night was also the first time that I saw my mother cry. I heard her tell Dad and Mim that the baby had a tumor that was "possibly cancer." I didn't fully grasp what that meant, but I sensed it was serious.

In the weeks that followed, neighbors took turns driving my mother to Children's Hospital each day after I left for school. Tisha was hospitalized for weeks with multiple surgeries and radiation treatments. I knew that she was very sick and might not live. I was scared for her. Yet, I was perhaps even more concerned about how our family had changed. My mother was preoccupied with her sick baby. She grew quiet, and I noticed her clothes began looking too large for her diminishing frame. Dad spent his evenings in quiet conversation with Mom. He still helped me with my homework, and we sometimes watched TV together, but we didn't laugh as much. Mim's days were consumed with caring for my three-year-old sister. Something sorrowful came over our house. Things improved some when Tisha came home from the hospital; still, she remained a sick baby, then a sick child. She and our family never fully recovered.

My sisters were much younger than I was, too young to be my playmates or confidants. It wasn't until they were almost adults that we connected. My baby sister, though, grew into my best friend. Tisha and I take beach vacations together to the Jersey shore for sister time, and we traveled to Italy, just she and I, to celebrate her sixtieth birthday. We talk on the phone daily to check in. We mourned the loss of our parents together, believing that no other human alive could completely share in or understand our pain. Coincidentally, it was Tisha who cared for me during my cancer treatment. She left her home in Maryland to stay with me in Pittsburgh for many weeks, driving me to radiation each day, at my side during chemotherapy, watching over me while I slept, waiting with my sons during my surgery, and sharing in the relief when I was pronounced cancer free. She's the sister every woman should have, perhaps more than I deserve.

Yet back when I was eleven, my baby sister's illness had turned my world upside down. Everything had changed, and I lost my sense of comfort as the center of my family's attention. I selfishly yearned to sit at the table in the kitchen of our old apartment on Larimer Avenue, where I ate breakfast each morning, where I did my homework after school, where Mom, Dad, and I had dinner when it was still just the three of us.

X
Ursula

I remember the last time I saw Ursula. My mother and I visited her at Pennsylvania Macaroni, the Italian grocery store in the Strip District where Ursula managed the cheese department. We found her behind the counter lifting large wheels of cheese, cutting off pieces with the huge cheese knife, and wrapping them in heavy white paper for waiting customers. She looked shrunken in stature as she aged. Her thinning brown hair was receding, and she had developed a protruding Adam's Apple. She looked like a little old man in a skirt. I filled Ursula in about my job and my kids while Mom bought a chunk of imported provolone and a sack of fresh mozzarella. Urs gave me a piece of cheese to sample, and we exchanged a smile that took me back to the days of putting the Chooch to bed. Back when Ursula's beer store was across the street from our Larimer Avenue apartment, when I went with her on summer evenings to store her cargo van for the night and walked home with my hand in hers.

When we moved to our apartment on Collins Avenue, Ursula came with us. She had been living with her younger brother, Victor. When he married, Victor's bride asked Ursula to leave, so my mother invited her to live with us. I liked having Ursula in the Collins Avenue house, like a part of the old neighborhood was still with us. Yet, it was her compassion that I loved most. Always supportive, never judgmental. Looking back, I suspect that her kindness may have grown partly from being denied it by others.

I'm unsure what financial arrangement she had with my parents, but Ursula frequently brought home bags filled with groceries—ground beef, sausage, vegetables, pasta, and tomatoes for sauce. Sometimes she brought flank steak or pork chops, an extravagance for a family that ate primarily one-pot dinners. Yet, Ursula never ate with us. She left early in the morning and returned home long after dinner and sometimes after my bedtime.

Occasionally, Ursula would spend some time with my mom and me on her day off. One Sunday afternoon, she took us to a miniature golf course and watched while Mom and I clumsily hit the balls along the green felt. I attempted to maneuver my ball around the little pond and through the tunnel under a windmill. Ursula cheered and clapped when I finally got the little white ball in the hole.

The first time I saw an airplane, I stood beside Ursula. Pittsburgh International Airport was still a novelty, and Ursula took my mom and me one summer evening to watch the planes take off and land from the airport's observation deck. Ursula kept her eyes peeled for an incoming plane.

"Look there," she said, arm raised, pointing to a spot through a break in the clouds. "That plane's coming in!"

I watched with excitement and wondered aloud if I'd ever be a passenger on an airplane.

"Sure, you will," Ursula said. "You'll go to lots of amazing places. You'll see."

One day, a year or so after we moved to Collins Avenue, Ursula and I ran into each other at the top of the third-floor steps. She slept in the back bedroom, and I had the large bright front room that overlooked the street. We chatted a bit, and then I asked her the question that still haunts me.

"Urs, why don't you have breasts like my mom?"

Ursula's pretty cream-colored blouse rested flat against her chest. I wondered why she didn't have a womanly appearance like my mom and Mim. I noticed some of the older girls at school who were showing the beginnings of breasts and curves, and although I was only ten, I knew that my body would be going through changes, so I was curious about Ursula's. Thinking back, I wonder why I didn't ask my mother about growing into womanhood, about Ursula and how she seemed different. Years later, Mom and I did have a conversation where she explained that Ursula was born a female biologically but began to exhibit increasingly masculine physical characteristics as she grew to adulthood. Mom guessed that Ursula may have had some hormone imbalance. As a ten-year-old, however, I must have trusted my friendship with Ursula enough to talk with her directly, to ask without realizing what was surely an imposing, insensitive question.

Ursula averted her eyes, and she was silent for a moment.

"I don't know," she whispered, looking down. Her shoulders slumped, and her lips pressed together.

I realized my question stung, and I had broached something too personal, perhaps painful. I was immediately sorry, but I felt uncomfortable and didn't know what else to say. We walked down the steps together in silence. Our easy familiarity faded some after that encounter. It didn't occur to me then that my curiosity would change our relationship, but I was no longer an innocent child who accepted Ursula without question or conclusion. She must have feared increasingly difficult discussions as I got older. After that incident, I saw less of Ursula. Without much conversation, she came and went from her third-floor bedroom, the door of which was always closed.

Later that year, Ursula moved out. I'm unsure if her move was prompted by the fact that Mom was pregnant and Ursula presumed that we would need more space or if Ursula needed a different kind of space. She had sold the beer store shortly after we left Larimer Avenue, taking the job at the Italian grocery, and I think she moved somewhere closer to her work. We didn't see as much of her after she moved, but once in a while, Ursula would stop by in the station wagon that she bought after the Chooch died, and she'd take my mother, my little sister, and me to get soft-serve ice cream or for an evening at Kennywood Park.

My contact with Ursula diminished as I got older—an occasional visit at my mom's, a quick hello in the Strip District store. Life was busy with a career, two sons, friends, and traveling to all the places she'd predicted I'd go. Thoughts of Ursula faded, so it was a surprise when I got the call from Mom.

"Ursula died," she said.

"Really? When? How did it happen?" I felt a fluttering in my stomach and pressed my hand to it.

Mom filled in the few details that she knew. Sudden. Perhaps a heart attack. She wasn't sure. "She always loved you," Mom said.

"I know."

"She asked about you every time I saw her."

There it was—the heartbreaking reminder that I hadn't been to see Ursula in a few years. I opened my mouth, but words wouldn't free themselves from my throat. My guilt smarted. Did I foolishly expect that Ursula would always be there? She had continued working at the store in the Strip District, and I thought about how many times I had passed by and not gone in to say hello. I felt ashamed that I allowed myself to take her for granted. Dear Ursula, who I'm certain would have never missed an opportunity to see me.

I can't know for sure if Ursula was happy back then. She may have been living the exact life that she wanted. What seemed to me as loneliness may have been an intense need for privacy, which I had broached all those years before. I wonder if Ursula had been born a couple of generations later if her life might have been slightly easier to navigate. Sadly, we still marginalize those who are viewed as different, yet I suspect that more support may be available today than in the 1950s. Either way, I wanted my Ursula to have been accepted for whatever non-conforming self she embodied and to have had the respect and support that she deserved.

I can't help but question if I had given her respect and support over the years. I ascribe no guilt to my curious ten-year-old self. Still, my adult self acknowledged that I, too, attempted to categorize Ursula and tried to unpack the mystery of her gender. Ultimately, the pure grief of losing her eclipsed any guilt I felt.

I was quiet while Mom reminisced about our decades-long friendship with Ursula. I waited until we hung up to let my tears flow.

XI

Neighborhood Boy

"It's not just for girls," I said as persuasively as I knew how.
Tommy sat on Grandma's front steps while I marked out hopscotch blocks in white chalk on the sidewalk.

"I'm not playing hopscotch," he insisted.

"Please. I really want you to."

Grandma's block was unusually quiet for a summer afternoon as Tommy walked to the sidewalk and looked up and down the street. "I'll play until someone comes out. Then I'm quitting."

Born ten days apart, Tommy and I shared a childhood more like brother and sister than cousins. We learned to walk at about the same time, played with my dolls and his toy soldiers on my living room floor, and later helped Grandma pick tomatoes from her backyard. Aunt Jo and Tommy lived on Grandma's third floor, and Tommy and I played for hours on her front porch and sidewalk. When we were five, we walked to kindergarten at Larimer School together. We shared a family and a neighborhood.

Aunt Jo wasn't Tommy's mother, but his grandmother. In the late 1940s, Aunt Jo's only daughter, an unmarried teenager, became pregnant. They did what many families in their situation did at the time: Aunt Jo raised Tommy as her own child. Tommy's mother married when she was in her early twenties and had six more children, but she never embraced Tommy as her own, and, as far as I knew, he didn't see much of her. As a kid, Tommy called Aunt Jo "Mom." I'm not sure when he—or I, for that matter—discovered that she was his grandmother, but by the time we were adolescents, he had switched to calling her "Jo."

Aunt Jo moved to Shadyside when Tommy and I were in first grade, and he transferred to Sacred Heart Elementary School. Grandma's third floor sat empty. Tommy and I no longer walked to school together and didn't even make our First Holy Communion together. We saw each other mostly on weekends, Saturday afternoons tossing a ball around on my side porch, and Sunday dinners in Grandma's kitchen. We spent holidays waving sparklers on Grandma's porch on the fourth of July, trick or treating on Halloween, he in a cowboy costume and I in my princess dress that Mim made, stopping at each house on Orphan and Whittier Streets.

Growing up, Tommy and I spent every Christmas sharing a mini sleepover with cousins at Grandma's on Christmas Eve. Then on Christmas day, we played with our new toys, made castles from Torrone candy boxes, and learned to juggle oranges from Grandma's fruit bowl. Later, when Tommy and I were about twelve and Christmas Eve had moved to Mim's, Tommy and Aunt Jo would come to our house on Collins Avenue Christmas Eve afternoon. While my mom and Aunt Jo prepared dishes to take to Mim's for dinner, Tommy and I would carry out our day-before-Christmas ritual. We'd use a premise like going for a walk to the park or getting a Coke as an excuse to leave. Then, we'd walk the two miles to Tommy's apartment in Shadyside, a cramped first-floor flat in a converted house on Shady Avenue.

Once there, Tommy would go straight to the living room and sit before the Christmas tree. He would reach under the tree and remove all his gifts, placing them on the floor in front of me. It was my job to carefully open each package so that I didn't ruin the paper or decoration and so that the Scotch tape could be reused. Then, Tommy would open each gift, pulling out sweaters, a baseball glove, and record albums. After he was satisfied, I would carefully rewrap each package to return it to its original spot under the tree. I thought it was a stupid exercise as it ruined any Christmas morning surprise, but Tommy thought it genius. I'm guessing he enjoyed knowing what was in the boxes, but I also think he relished my complicity in his secret.

Tommy and I saw less of each other as we grew into our teenage years. I overheard Aunt Jo telling my mom that Tommy often didn't come home at night, that he was secretive, that he was sometimes abrupt with her when she questioned him, and that she worried about him. Tommy's behavior seemed to be fueled by an increasingly rebellious nature, while I lacked the courage to do anything other than follow the rules.

In our early teens, Tommy was sent to Thorn Hill School, a facility for "delinquent boys" remanded there by the county juvenile court. Thorn Hill was situated on 1,500 acres about twenty miles north of Pittsburgh. In an agricultural environment, boys lived in group cottages and worked at farming chores. I saw Tommy only on occasional visits home. He looked healthy, tanned from being outdoors. On one visit, he attempted to make light of his situation, telling me how he enjoyed working on the farm and caring for the chickens. Tommy had a pet cow that I think he named Betty. It annoys me all these years later that I can't be sure about the name of that cow. My annoyance turns to anger, perhaps because it's too late to ask him.

I'm not sure what deed Tommy committed to be sent to Thorn Hill. I didn't ask many questions back then. I just listened to what he wanted to tell me. I thought about our strange twist of circumstance. He, who had always seemed free, now confined in a youth correction facility, and I, usually confined by my adherence to rules and conformity, now free to enjoy my teen years. At Peabody High School, I joined clubs, served as an officer in my sorority, hung out with friends, and went to dances. The odd thing is that during his stay at Thorn Hill, Tommy seemed relaxed, quick to smile, content.

Like so many lost details, I can't recall how long Tommy stayed at Thorn Hill—it could have been months or years—but at some point after he returned, he asked me to take him for a driving test. We were about eighteen then, and I had been driving for over a year.

I pulled my Dodge Dart into the parking lot of the public housing high-rise where Aunt Jo and Tommy had moved. He came through the door, hair a bit longer than when I last saw him, wearing jeans and a black tee shirt with a Jefferson Airplane image.

"Hey, what's up?" he asked as he walked toward the car. He came around to the driver's side and opened the door. "I'll drive," he said.

"Do you know how?" I asked.

"Sure," he replied. "It can't be that hard."

I suggested we ride through Highland Park to decide if he was ready for the test. I urged him to practice parallel parking and three-point turns. Instead, Tommy drove down Washington Boulevard, The Stones screaming from the radio, "Can't Get No Satisfaction," while we cruised through Eat n' Park. While he went faster than I felt comfortable, he clearly knew how to drive.

When we stopped at a red light, my eyes fell on his hand resting on the steering wheel, and I noticed a tattoo. "TOM" was engraved in large case block letters across the top of his hand just above the knuckles. I stared at the blue-black ink against his pale skin, the letters expanding when he grasped the steering wheel.

"What's that?" I asked, pointing to his hand.

"Cool, isn't it?"

I didn't respond. I thought the tattoo peculiar and wondered what prompted him to have this name etched in ink on his hand. Who is TOM? I wondered. He was always Tommy to the family and me. I studied the TOM tattoo, and it seemed to challenge me, as if to say, *See, he's different. You don't know him anymore.*

We pulled into the State Police parking lot and entered the testing station to register. I sat in the waiting room while Tommy and an officer got in my car and pulled away. It wasn't long before they returned, Tommy looking annoyed.

"He failed me," Tommy said, nodding over his shoulder toward the officer. Tommy explained that he failed the exam, not because of poor driving skills but because he couldn't correctly answer the questions on the oral part of the test. We spent the next few days studying the driver's manual—how far to park from a stop sign, what to do when encountering a flashing signal, and rules on merging. Tommy and I returned to the testing station the following week, and he passed the exam. We celebrated with a double order of Eat n' Park french fries.

It was around the mid-1960s when Aunt Jo and Tommy returned to our Larimer neighborhood, living in a small apartment in a ten-floor public housing high rise at the corner of Larimer and Auburn Street, about eight blocks and many worlds from where Tommy and I were born. The 1960s were a turning point for Larimer Avenue. Many homeowners left the old neighborhood and moved to the suburbs, creating disinvestment in home ownership and leaving behind rentals with absentee landlords. Homes where my old neighbors had lived began to deteriorate. Within a few years, many local businesses, like Labriola's Market and Moio's Bakery, moved their stores to the suburbs, and some buildings sat vacant. A different kind of crime took over as drug dealers replaced the guys on the stoop.

As Italian immigrants left Larimer Avenue, African Americans moved in, uprooted by urban development in other parts of the city. Some Italian families felt threatened by this shift in population, accelerating their flight to the suburbs. As part of a vast redevelopment program, entire blocks of houses in our old neighborhood were demolished and replaced by low-income housing. The community atmosphere disappeared as strangers crowded into high rises. This was the Larimer Avenue that Tommy returned to.

At about this time, I graduated from high school and got a job working in the Customer Service Department at Sears. I dressed meticulously for work each day in a pleated miniskirt and matching sweater. I saved enough from my paycheck to visit an upscale salon in East Liberty to have my hair cut from the collar-length flip style I had worn in high school into a pixie cut like Twiggy, the famous English model. I considered myself grown up and independent. Yet, I had a strict curfew of ten p.m. on work nights and midnight on weekends. When I turned twenty-one, I still lived at home, sheltered by my dad's rules and restrictions, disconnected from the decline of my old neighborhood.

I seldom saw Tommy back then, and I don't know what his life was like. Looking back, I mourn what I didn't know. I hate the gaps in my memory. I missed Tommy in a way similar to how I missed our old neighborhood, recognizing that what I longed for no longer existed.

Tommy moved to Florida when we were in our twenties. I overheard comments between Mom and Mim that he was using drugs. I don't know what substance Tommy was consuming, likely more than smoking weed. Perhaps he was into the hallucinogens popular with hippies in the early 1970s. Yet, I doubt he was truly part of the counterculture, rejecting tradition and distrusting the government. Somehow, I can't picture him participating in civil rights sit-ins or marches protesting the war in Vietnam. I suspect that his dropping out was more personal. Perhaps he gave up on a life without parents, without a neighborhood, and without a clear sense of identity. Or maybe Tommy didn't escape but was left behind. Either way, I'm not sure if I realized at the time that we were losing him.

I saw Tommy only on a few occasions when he returned to Pittsburgh for a brief visit. He was home one afternoon when Mom, Mim, and I visited Aunt Jo. He avoided eye contact and didn't talk much; our once-easy conversation became awkward. He seemed anxious, pacing Aunt Jo's living room barefoot, his hair down to his shoulders, his movements jerky, his eyes darting. We weren't there long when Tommy retreated to his room and shut the door. I was frightened for him but never spoke of it to anyone, maybe in an attempt to protect myself from confronting the truth.

One weekend in the spring of 1974, a couple of months after our twenty-seventh birthday, Tommy came home unexpectedly. He called my mother one evening asking about me, telling her that he wanted to see me, that it was important. When I got the message the next morning and called Aunt Jo's apartment, Tommy had already left for Florida. A couple of days later, he was dead.

I overheard family members whispering the word "overdose." Aunt Jo told everyone that Tommy had died of a heart attack. Mim told me the truth. I learned that the coroner's report indicated evidence that Tommy had shot heroin under each fingernail and toenail, or perhaps it was between his fingers and toes. I later understood that this practice was an attempt by heroin addicts to hide track marks. I wondered what pain Tommy was trying to numb. I suspected that the overdose was likely intentional. Certain that he had come home to say goodbye, I foolishly convinced myself that I could have saved him.

A few days later, Mom, Mim, and I walked into DeRosa's funeral home, where my family had said goodbye to aunts, uncles, and Grandma. The entrance hall was crowded with the familiar faces of family and friends. My eyes fell on a small black felt sign with white lettering spelling Tommy's last name, indicating his room. Mom and Mim went ahead; I waited near the door. The aroma of roses and lilies overpowered any fresh air, and I suddenly felt queasy. Someone passed, bumping my arm; someone else asked if I was okay. I wasn't.

I don't remember walking into the room where Tommy lay in his casket; somehow, I was standing before him. I ignored the buzz of conversation around me, focusing on his face posed in a peaceful expression, head resting on a satin pillow. Aunt Jo had asked Mike DeRosa to cut and style Tommy's hair into a pompadour reminiscent of the 1950s and to dress him in a grey suit and white shirt with a tie. I think seeing TOM in the casket would have been easier. I turned and ran outside without speaking to anyone.

My dad's cousin, Emory, a priest and pastor of Help of Christians Church, said the funeral Mass two days later. I have little recollection of the service except for the casket in front of the altar.

I can't remember what I felt.

When we left the church, I rode in the back seat of Uncle's car with Mom and Mim; Dad sat in the front with Uncle. We entered Mount Carmel Cemetery—where my ancestors were buried, and most of my relatives would later be buried—and parked along the road a few cars behind the hearse. We walked to a spot that had been roped off around an empty grave with a metal stand hovering above, waiting for the casket, waiting for Tommy. Chairs lined each side, and I chose one in the first row, closest to the open grave. His coffin arrived, carried by some of my male cousins and one of my uncles, and Emory gave the blessing, words I can't remember but that somehow seemed to comfort Aunt Jo and the rest of the family.

The graveside service ended, and Emory instructed everyone to return to their cars. I refused. I couldn't leave Tommy alone, resting in a satin-lined wooden box atop a deep hole in the ground. It felt like abandonment. He wouldn't have left me, I reasoned to myself. I sat affixed to the hard wooden folding chair while family and friends walked slowly back to their cars.

"Linda, it's time to go," Emory whispered. He took my hand, his other hand grasping my shoulder, and attempted to lift me from my seat.

I held firm. "I'm not leaving him."

"You're not really leaving him. He will live on with you."

Typical priest nonsense, I thought. I didn't respond but remained eyes fixed on Tommy's casket, feet planted in the grass.

"Why don't you just take him with you? Pull him into your heart and hold him there."

The sobs—fierce and surging—came from deep in my chest. Emory sat patiently, holding my hand until I had exhausted myself. Then he walked me to the car, where Mim waited and gathered me into her arms. Tommy died long before 1974. I mourned him, but it was TOM that we buried that day. TOM, who I never really knew.

I remember the last time I saw Tommy. It was the year before he died, and he was in town for a few days. He called and asked me if I wanted to hang out for a while, something we hadn't done in a long time. I picked him up at Aunt Jo's and almost didn't recognize him when he walked from the building toward the car. He was thin, his face sullen. His stringy brown hair, limp past his shoulders, looked unwashed. He wore stained jeans and Jesus sandals covering dirty feet.

Thankfully, Tommy's mood lifted as we started driving. We spent the afternoon together riding around, making our usual stop for french fries, and singing along to Led Zeppelin and The Doors on my car radio. Laughing and reminiscing, our differences dissolved. No longer a married, working mother and a strung-out drug addict, we were kids again, playing hopscotch on Grandma's sidewalk.

Tommy and me on Grandma's front steps.

XII

Norma and Dan

I've heard this story often: In December of the first year my parents were married, Mom arranged a surprise birthday party for Dad at my grandmother's house with Mom's sisters and brothers and their spouses and kids. Mim decorated the dining room with blue and yellow paper streamers. Uncle Richard went through his collection of jazz records and chose a few of his favorites to play, while Aunt Gilda and Uncle Bob selected bottles of homemade red wine and carried them up from the basement. Grandma had made two cakes that afternoon—one small round one that she decorated for the singing of Happy Birthday and the other, a plain sheet cake, as a backup to feed the large crowd. Uncle Glen handed out party hats to the kids as a bribe for them to hide quietly behind the sofa. Aunt Edith was posted in the front room as the lookout, and she signaled to the others as my parents approached the house.

"Surprise!" Everyone yelled when Mom and Dad walked through the front door.

Dad was so overcome that he had to step back onto the front porch. Through tears, he told Mom this was his first birthday party. He was twenty-nine.

An orphan by age ten, Dad was left alone and vulnerable, a situation that carved out lifelong roles for my parents—Dad, wounded, and Mom, nurturing. I remember a Saturday afternoon when I was in my forties, and I had stopped by my parents' duplex for a visit. I found Dad alone, sitting in his well-worn green recliner and watching Pirates baseball on TV. Mom was shopping with friends, and Dad remarked that he hadn't had lunch yet. When I asked why, he replied, "She wasn't here to feed me." What was even more ridiculous about Dad's statement was that I didn't question it.

Mom was the quintessential nurturer and thrived on being needed, with much of her caregiving centered around food. She made eggplant parmigiana for her family doctor and took it to appointments, kept snacks in her refrigerator for neighborhood kids, and volunteered at the senior center behind her house in Morningside, serving food to elderly folks, most of whom were younger than Mom. "Are you hungry?" was Mom's first question when you walked through her door. She expressed disappointment if you told her that you had just eaten. "Oh," she'd say with a sigh. "Are you sure you don't want something? I made stuffed shells and meatballs." In her passive, unassuming way, Mom was good at dispensing guilt, and before you knew how it happened, you were sitting at her dining room table with a plate of stuffed shells.

Dad relied on Mom's care. It almost seemed she had trained him to require it, simultaneously meeting both their needs. Once in their later years, Mom told me that she hoped Dad would die before her.

"Why would you want that?" I asked.

"Because he wouldn't do well alone," she replied.

"But I'd have him come live with me. I'd take care of him," I said.

Mom smiled. "You have no idea. He's like a kid needing care. I think it's because he didn't have a mother growing up."

That Saturday afternoon, I knew my father could make himself something to eat, but I went into the kitchen and fixed him an omelet. We sat together at the dining room table while he ate. I don't remember why or how, but the topic of my father's long-ago illness came up. Dad didn't often talk about his time in the tuberculous hospital, but I asked him about it that day. He explained that after his surgery, he spent almost two years in the Leech Farm Tuberculosis Sanitarium on a hillside in the East End. He told me about how the patients slept outside on the porch year-round, even in the middle of winter, because of the belief that tuberculosis germs couldn't multiply in the cold. "It was damn cold out there," he said. "We each had only one thin blanket." Dad's friends stopped by occasionally, but their visits dropped off after the first few months. Dad's brother Nick visited once a month or so, but his sister Irene came every week, bringing homemade cookies and cakes she shared with the nurses and patients who had no visitors.

I had always wondered why Dad stayed so long in the tuberculosis hospital. "Did it take two years to get better?" I asked.

"Well, not really," Dad said. He described how after about a year or so, he had recovered enough that the doctors said he could go home. "I told my brother Nick that the doctors thought I might be able to leave, but I didn't know where to go. Nick said I could live with him and Mary until I got on my feet." They made plans for Nick to pick Dad up the following Sunday.

That week, Dad packed his few clothes, said goodbye to his fellow patients, and thanked the nurses and doctors. Sunday came, and he sat on the side of his bed on the porch, waiting. A worn leather suitcase that he had acquired from a patient who died the month before was at his feet. Nick never came. And he didn't come the following Sunday or the Sunday after that. Nick didn't visit again. It turned out that Mary was afraid to bring a tuberculosis patient into their home with two small children. Dad seemed to understand her fear.

"When Nick didn't come for me, I realized I was a burden," Dad said. "I didn't want to be a problem for Irene too, so I never said anything to her. I lied and said that the doctors decided I wasn't ready to go home after all."

Dad stayed at the sanitarium for several more months until one day, when Irene was visiting, one of the nurses told her it was a shame that Danny couldn't find a place to go home. "He's been ready to leave for a while now," the nurse said.

Irene was furious and arranged for my dad to go home with her that week. Irene and her husband had a baby of their own, but there was no way she was letting her little brother spend one more day in that place than he had to.

I can't imagine a patient today being permitted to stay in a hospital longer than necessary. I assume that in 1937, indigent patients were cared for under FDR's New Deal with publicly funded health care. I think of Dad as a twenty-one-year-old and can't help but wonder if he found security living in a tuberculosis hospital, feeling safety that was likely unattainable for him in the outside world.

When he met Mom, it was no wonder that Dad found her big, warm, family inviting, and it must have been part of his attraction to her. My mother grew up with two loving parents, a stable home with plenty of food, and the camaraderie of nine siblings. She lived with her large family in a four-bedroom house with a big backyard and a second kitchen in the basement where my grandmother baked bread and prepared homemade pasta. My grandfather, who died when Mom was twenty, was an opera aficionado who played his recordings of *Aida* and *Turandot* on a Victrola phonograph in the family living room.

It also didn't hurt that Mom was pretty, the kind of pretty that smiles from the cover of a 1940s magazine. She was small, just five foot two inches, and slim with dark wavy hair that fell to her shoulders. She was quick with a pleasant smile and easily made friends with strangers. In the 1980s, when I worked as a property manager, I remember a woman came to my office looking for an apartment. "Your mother sent me," she explained. I asked if she was a friend of Mom's. "Not really," the woman replied. "I met her on the bus yesterday." This was typical of Mom, and I think her outgoing disposition was part of what attracted Dad.

I suspect Mom was drawn to Dad's quiet strength, kindness, and good looks. Dad matched the stereotype of tall, dark, and handsome: slim but strong, six foot with thick dark hair, hazel eyes, and a shy crooked smile that endeared him to almost everyone he met. While they made a good-looking pair, their distinct personalities might have made them seem an unlikely couple. While Dad fancied reading and Scrabble, Mom was energetic and usually couldn't sit long enough to finish a novel. Dad was introspective—a thinker. Mom was a doer. Yet, they meshed perfectly where it counted. Mom responded to Dad's wounds, and she thrived on being needed. Despite outward appearances of strength, my dad carried the baggage of emptiness, and Mom filled the void.

Mom wasn't much of a storyteller, not like Dad or me. I had to probe and pry stories from her. One day over a cup of coffee at her dining room table, I asked how she and Dad met. Like many couples, my parents met through friends. Mom's best friend, Jenny, was dating Chuck, a young man from Dad's Homewood-Brushton neighborhood. Jenny and Chuck set up a blind date with Norma and Dan. I can imagine the scene of their first date—Mom doing most of the talking, Dad listening, smiling. The foursome developed a close friendship. It was the summer of 1945, and the war was ending. In January of 1946, Jenny and Chuck married, with my parents serving as their maid of honor and best man. In April of that year, Jenny and Chuck returned the honors when my mom and dad married.

My parents' wedding photo sits on my bookcase in an eight-by-ten wooden frame. Mom, her dark hair in tight curls perfectly surrounding her face, a single strand of pearls sitting above the neckline of her gown, a large bouquet of white roses in her arm. Dad, handsome in his tux with white tie and carnation pinned to his lapel. They're smiling with closed lips, looking afar at some spot out of the camera's eye—the start of a life together.

Mom and Dad moved into the Larimer Avenue apartment where I was born eleven months later at the beginning of the post-war baby boom. My parents had an agreement about naming their first child. Mom would select a boy's name, and Dad would choose a girl's. When I was born, a popular song by Buddy Guy called "Linda" filled the airwaves. My dad liked the song, so Linda was the name he chose. I always sensed that Dad enjoyed being the source of my name, and he sang the song to me often at bedtime. I don't have particular feelings one way or the other about my name, but the fact that it was my dad's choice feels like a treasured gift. Like my mother often reminded me, I've always been my father's daughter.

Naming me may have been the only decision my mother conceded to Dad throughout their marriage. For most of my parents' life together, Mom was in charge. She made family decisions about where we lived; she paid the bills, strategically stretching Dad's meager paycheck; she arranged their social life, which primarily involved visiting with Mom's family. Often, Mom didn't tell Dad about decisions until after they were made, like when she found their rental in Morningside and decided to move. She had so much chutzpah that sometimes she tried to convince Dad that he had contributed to decisions that he knew nothing about.

In 1970, my parents moved into their duplex on Chislett Street in the working-class neighborhood of Morningside. While the inside was small, it had a decent-sized front porch with bright green synthetic outdoor carpet, a few webbed aluminum folding chairs, and old TV trays. It was there on the porch where my mother held court, greeting passing neighbors, visiting with her lady friends from card club or church, and feeding cookies and juice boxes to the neighborhood kids. In a community of single-family homes, Mom viewed the duplex as an improvement in their living situation that called for some upgrades in their furnishings. Her priority was to replace the old dining room table that Aunt Edith had given her years before. My parents certainly didn't have the cash to buy new furniture, and Dad didn't believe in buying on credit. "If you don't have the money to buy what you want, then save up for it," was his motto. Ironically, Mom worked part-time in the credit department at Sears and was frustrated that she couldn't open her own account there. In the early 1970s, a married woman needed her husband's signature to apply for credit.

One evening, Mom called me and asked if I would drive her to Horne's Department Store in the East Hills Shopping Center. They were having a furniture sale, and she secretly wanted to look for a dining room table and chairs. When I asked her how she'd buy furniture if Dad didn't agree to buy on credit, she said, "I'll figure something out."

The next evening, Mom and I walked through an assortment of sofas, end tables, and buffets until we came upon the dining room tables and chairs. Mom examined each one, looking at the price tag and then moving to the next. Finally, she arrived at an olive-green laminate table with sculpted curved ends. It came with six matching and equally unattractive olive-green chairs.

"Look," she said, turning to me, "This one's on sale!"

A salesman approached, and he and Mom gushed in unison over the table. "Do you have an account with us?" the salesman asked.

"Not yet," Mom replied.

I admired her conviction but wondered aloud, "Mom, how will you work this out with Dad?"

"Don't worry," she said. Somehow, I had confidence in her.

Mom talked with the salesman while I wandered through the aisles of furniture. Finally, she was ready to return home. "Can you bring Dad and me back here tomorrow evening?" she asked. Assuming Mom wanted me along for some perceived moral support, I said I would. Plus, I didn't want to miss this scene playing out.

The next evening, Mom, Dad, and I returned to Horne's under some premise I can't now remember. Mom strolled through the store, gravitating toward the furniture department, with Dad obediently and unassumingly following. She skillfully meandered toward the dining room tables.

"Oh, look, Dan. They have tables on sale! We should just take a look."

"No need to look if we're not buying," Dad replied.

"Oh, come on. It doesn't cost anything to look." Mom made her way toward the green eyesore. Dad followed dutifully while I observed with wonder and admiration. You had to hand it to her.

"Oh, this one's pretty," Mom said, stroking the faux wood green tabletop. "I wonder if it's on sale."

Dad reached for the tag hanging from the bottom of the table to see the price. "Hold for Schifino," it read.

"God dammit, woman! What did you do?" Dad was angry.

Realizing that her charade was exposed, Mom started to giggle nervously. I watched in amazement, expecting my father to storm off any minute. Instead, he slowly shook his head back and forth, looking down at the tag with his name, and began to chuckle.

This was a man who recognized when he was outdone.

Dad agreed to buy the table and chairs on credit, saying later that he'd come to realize that he and Mom might as well join the rest of America putting themselves in debt.

My parents' marriage wasn't perfect. They argued, sometimes about spending money, often about going out to socialize. Mom always craving more, and Dad preferring less. Their disagreements never seemed serious, more like bickering. What I imagine most couples do. Looking back, it appeared that Mom usually won the arguments. I suspect that she just wore Dad down. Yet, they worked it out, and my guess is that it never occurred to either of them to do otherwise.

As a young adult, I admired my parents' ability to determine how a marriage worked. Something I never quite figured out myself. Something my generation wasn't very good at. I wondered what gave them such regard for the institution of marriage. Was it the war? Seeing most of the world in upheaval might have made their generation crave marriage and family stability. Perhaps long-ingrained cultural norms caused them to accept marriage without question. I can't imagine that my parents knew anyone who was divorced. Or maybe it was religion. My mother's devotion to the Catholic church would have prevented her from ever considering breaking her marriage vows. Of course, I don't want to overlook that Mom and Dad loved each other. Their devotion was palpable in her compassion for his difficult childhood and how she tried to make up for it, in the way he acquiesced to her, with gentleness and good humor. But I suspect that some element of their commitment was also generational. Somehow, their generation's worldview garnered a dedication to relationships, sticking it out, and keeping commitments.

Still, while there's something to be admired in my parents' devotion to each other, I can't help but blame their generation for defining gender in limiting terms. Too often, women were relegated to supporting roles and limited options, particularly those like me who were stuck in bad marriages. Living with cultural, political, and economic inequality, too many wives felt trapped in marriages with men who abused them, who drank too much like my first husband, who disrespected them and saw them as less than. So, this was the rub—what my generation struggled with—how to marry dedication with equality.

Fortunately, my parents seemed to have fashioned an equilibrium of empowerment. Dad was content to allow Mom to take the lead on most things. In return, he was nurtured to the point of almost complete indulgence. She cooked what he wanted, ate when he chose, then spent evenings watching the TV shows he preferred. Dad became more sedentary as he aged, while Mom's energy almost seemed to increase with time. Into her eighties, Mom continued to walk five long blocks to and from church, took Tai Chi classes at the Senior Center, and was always ready for an afternoon visiting with friends or shopping. Except when Dad asked her to stay home with him. Then she gladly surrendered her freedom in favor of what she undoubtedly viewed as her life's purpose.

Mom and Dad wedding photo.

XIII

Searching for the Sweetness

I walked in the door of my neighborhood Dunkin' Donuts and was immediately immersed in the familiar aroma. I was here for my weekly Saturday morning allotment—one classic glazed donut. Since I was a toddler, donuts have been my go-to bakery snack. I've always preferred the light yeasty taste of a raised donut. Sweet, but not too sweet, chewy, fluffy, and sticky with glaze. No cake donuts for me, no colored sprinkles, no jelly or cream filling, no fruity flavors. Only the traditional raised donut would do. It suited me, not unlike my personality—pleasing but not exceptionally sweet, unpretentious, classic.

My love of donuts has a long history. When I was in my thirties and my two sons were small, we lived just three blocks from my parents' duplex on Chislett Street. Stagno's Bakery was just a couple of blocks away. Every Saturday morning, we stopped at Stagno's, where the boys would select donuts to take to my parents. They knew what to order; Mom and Dad preferred the cake type, and the boys liked ones with sprinkles. I wanted the sticky classic glazed.

My older son carried the white bakery box tied with string up the steps to my parents' front porch.

"We're here," I called into the dining room as we came in the front door.

"And we have donuts!" one of the boys yelled.

We all sat around the dining room table with its green vinyl tablecloth, the donut box occupying a place at the center. Mom poured coffee for herself and me, and Dad passed around paper plates. We munched our donuts, Dad and the boys washing theirs down with milk. My sons started calling the ritual "donut day," and it stuck.

One Saturday morning in July, Mom was cleaning up crumbs from under the boys' chairs while Dad ate his second cake donut. I fidgeted with my napkin and shifted my weight in my chair, anxious and anticipating a difficult conversation with my parents. I took a gulp of coffee, left my sons sitting at the table, and asked Mom and Dad to move into the living room to talk.

My parents appeared surprised at the news that I was getting a divorce. We never talked about his drinking. They didn't seem to want to notice, and I didn't want to discuss it. As far as I knew, they thought he was a nice guy, a husband for their daughter and a father for their grandsons. Beyond that, I'm not sure what they saw. I never told them how he pushed the kids around. I never told them about the time when he had his hands around my throat while I lay on my back on the kitchen floor of our Beacon Street townhouse, him hovering over me. I didn't tell them about the time when I had my hands around his throat as he lay in an alcohol numbness passed out on our bed. The suppressed memory of that day came into focus. Coming home from errands. Unable to find my two-year-old. Searching desperately, frantically through the neighborhood. Feeling relief when I found him almost an hour later. Then rage.

My dad released me from the memory when he asked if I was okay.

"Yeah, Daddy, I'm fine."

"You don't need to say anything to anyone." These were the first words that my mother spoke.

"What do you mean not say anything to anyone?" I asked. "What am I supposed to do, pretend I'm still married?"

My mother stressed over what the family would think, what the neighbors would think, what her card club would think, what the Christian Mothers at Saint Raphael's Church would think. Mom was likely also concerned about the stigma that divorce still held in 1980, at least for her generation.

I gathered the boys, donut crumbs in their hands and sprinkles still on their faces, and I left my parents' house abruptly. I got in my car and drove home. I might have been speeding, hands tight on the wheel, furious at my mother's betrayal, but perhaps even more enraged that she had tarnished my sweetest memory of her.

When I was about two years old, my mom worked evenings part-time at Nabisco when it was still called the National Biscuit Company. Mom worked along the conveyor belt, where she and her co-workers removed the passing cookies and crackers and packaged them in cartons. At the end of their shift, employees were allowed to take home products that had broken while traveling along the belt. When Mom's shift was finished, she went to the end of the conveyer where pieces of cookies, bits of crackers, and fragments of other baked goods had collected in a bin. She took a few handfuls of the tasty morsels and put them in one of the paper bags her employer generously provided. Mom liked to refer to the mismatched assortment of broken baked goods as donuts.

Mom walked the six blocks down Larimer Avenue and up the stairs to our second-floor apartment when her work was over. As she came through the kitchen door, she held up the bag of treats. I sat in my highchair, where my dad had given me dinner, and I played with my little doll while he cleaned the kitchen.

"There's little Linda," Mom said, smiling, and I let out a happy squeal. She quickly said hello to Dad, standing at the sink drying dishes, then took her coat off and hung it on the back of one of the metal-legged chairs with yellow vinyl seats. Then Mom turned her attention to me.

"Do you know what I have for you?"

"Donuts!"

Mom pulled up one of the kitchen chairs to face me and opened the paper bag. I can still smell the aroma that escaped as she reached inside and removed some of the so-called donuts. Mom held out one of the treats, and I grabbed it with my chubby hands. We giggled and took turns nibbling as she produced each delicious nugget, me getting crumbs on my face and licking them from my fingers. None of my enduring memories of my mother are as tender as this one.

Later, when I was five or six and Mom had left her brief stint at Nabisco, she began making actual donuts. Mom gathered ingredients and pulled a small stool up to the kitchen counter so that I could watch. She heated milk on the stove, poured it into a bowl, and mixed in the yeast. I'd lean over the bowl to take in the pungent yeasty fragrance. I watched every step while Mom added eggs, butter, flour, and sugar, blending the ingredients into a dough. Then, she moved the mixture to the kitchen table to begin the kneading, pushing the heels of her palms into the dough over and over, sprinkling flour, and then massaging it some more. Once Mom was satisfied that the dough was ready, she rested it in a bowl covered with a dish towel. After it rose sufficiently, Mom rolled out the dough on the floured tabletop. Then came the part where I helped.

Standing on my stool, I used a metal cutter, pressing it into the dough to shape donuts with small holes in the center. Mom watched over my shoulder, offering instructions. "Put the cuts closer together so we get more donuts. Don't twist the cutter, or you'll tear the dough." Mom fried the formed donuts in a heavy skillet to a crispy finish. She used a sugar glaze to top some and left others plain. When the donuts were finished, Dad and I sat at the kitchen table and ate them while they were still warm. I liked the taste of Mom's homemade donuts. Still, somehow this experience never aroused the same sensation as those early days sitting in the highchair across from Mom, feeling completely loved.

This is the mother that I searched for when I went to my parents' house that Saturday morning. Determined to escape a horrible marriage, yet fearful of the unknown, raising my sons, and living alone for the first time. I yearned for that long-ago warmth, from the donuts, from my mother.

I struggled to swallow my anger as I parked in front of my house. The boys and I were no sooner inside when I saw my father's Chevy Citation pull up behind my car. He slowly got out and lumbered up the steps to the front door where I was waiting.

"Are you okay, babe?"

"Yeah, Daddy, I'm fine."

"Don't listen to your mother," he said. "Do what's best for you."

"I will."

"You know that she cares about you, right?"

"Yeah, Daddy, I know."

Weeks went by.

My husband moved into the apartment I found for him. I changed the locks on what was now my house. My young sons and I settled in alone, happy, and safe. I knew that speaking of my situation with anyone would infuriate my mother, so I didn't tell anyone about the separation. I didn't say anything to the neighbors. I especially didn't say anything to my family except for Mim, of course, who wrapped me in her arms, whispering assurances that I'd be okay. I continued to see my parents each Saturday morning, but our visits felt superficial, an unnatural air hanging about their dining room as artificial as my mother's flowers. No one asked why my marriage was ending and what went wrong. Perhaps it was generational, and they thought it too private to inquire. For whatever reason, they didn't ask, and I didn't offer.

Months went by.

On a chilly fall Saturday morning, I arrived with the boys at my parents' house for another donut day. We entered the dining room, donut box in hand, to find my father's sister, Irene, sitting at the table. After hugs and greetings, she asked if my husband was joining us. My mother came through the kitchen door holding a pot of coffee and positioned herself behind Aunt Irene, shaking her head back and forth so hard that I thought she'd give herself a concussion. Mom glared at me with narrowed eyes, her mouth set in a hard line. I plopped the bakery box in the middle of the table.

"We're separated and getting a divorce," I said.

Mom looked defeated and walked back into the kitchen.

"Oh, that's too bad, honey," Aunt Irene said. "Are you okay?"

"Yeah, Aunt Irene. I'm fine."

She got up from her chair and enveloped me in a long hug saying, "Come here and let me give you some love."

Aunt Irene's affection was comforting, but the contrast with my mother's complete lack of support stung. My throat closed, and my stomach tightened. I sat at the table sipping coffee but couldn't eat my donut.

*　*　*

My mom wasn't always insensitive. There was a time that I looked to her to mend my wounds. The first injury I remember was a gash on my left knee.

It happened when I was five or six years old and walking with my mother on Orphan Street along the side of Ursula's store. I let go of Mom's hand and ran ahead when my foot caught a crack in the pavement. I should have held on to her. I fell on a piece of green glass, and it stuck in my knee. Mom pulled the glass out and took me home to care for my injury. She washed the cut clean, carefully applied mercurochrome, and then bandaged my knee. She examined, cleaned, reapplied, and re-bandaged each day. I felt bathed in mercurochrome embraces, nursed, and swaddled.

Mom was always good at caring for physical injuries. She nursed me with homemade chicken pastina soup and warm blankets through childhood colds, measles, and chicken pox. She watched over me when, as a teenager, I was diagnosed with a painful ovarian cyst that ultimately required surgery. Mom sat by my hospital bed, vigilant, holding the straw from a plastic cup of water to my mouth, adjusting my pillow, and cleaning my face when I threw up.

Yet, Mom fell short of caring for my emotional pain. When I grew older, there were times that it didn't seem to matter to her if I was hurt, sad, or struggling. It was Mim that I went to when my middle-school crush didn't reciprocate, and later when I realized there was no money for college, and I had to find a job after high school graduation to help at home. Mom didn't seem to have the capacity to give emotional comfort, nor did she seem to need it in return. She appeared to have developed a stoicism that she required from me as well.

When Dad died, I felt overwhelmed by the pain of his loss, and when Mom asked me to give the eulogy, my first response was, "Sorry, Mom, but I can't possibly find the strength." Still, she pressured me to speak at Dad's funeral, saying it would mean a lot to her. Mom knew I was a confident public speaker, but she also had to have known this was different. Dad's death crushed me. Despite this, I wrote a eulogy that I hoped would honor the father I adored and struggled to deliver it.

After the church service, I asked Mom if my words were good enough and if they comforted her.

"Oh," she said, "I don't know. I wasn't paying attention." It felt like a final jab as though she said, "*Here, you do it. After all, you were each other's favorite.*"

Over the years, I've convinced myself that perhaps she simply wanted family and friends to hear her daughter with a degree in rhetoric—her way of showing off.

I sometimes felt sorry for Mom and her seemingly never-ending struggle for admiration, for her constant efforts to create the appearance of a perfect family. It must have been exhausting. Now that my sons are grown, I understand how challenging it can be to parent adult children. How an urgency to protect them takes over when things aren't going well. How bad decisions happen. My mom guarded the family's reputation like a bobcat. She would lie, manipulate, and stage-manage whatever she deemed necessary to keep the family at peace or at least maintain the appearance of harmony. I can't imagine myself going to this extreme, but it scares me that I recognize the potential.

You'd never guess it on meeting her, but Mom had inner toughness. This is who you'd want on your team when your back was against the wall. She also valued loyalty. At Mom's funeral, several women came to me, remarking that they had lost their best friend. Amazing. I thought of my own few lifelong friendships. Others seem to come and go with marriages, career paths, and neighborhoods. I admired Mom's gift of sustaining enduring friendships, yet I was envious of these women and their closeness with Mom.

My mother was complex. Stubborn protector of family and traditions, yet resilient when necessary. Nurturing, but at times callous. She approached motherhood like it was her job—diligent, responsible, thorough, like any good employee. I'll bet that her boss at Nabisco was sorry to see her leave. Yet, occupations invite emotional detachment, and Mom cultivated hers. I wonder if my sister Tisha's illness caused Mom to create this distance. Had she learned from necessity to shield herself from pain? Or perhaps she was just spent. Either way, it saddens me that she lost her sweetness, and our closeness diminished in the process. I wonder if she, too, felt the loss.

***

I stood at the Dunkin' Donuts counter surveying the trays along the back wall, even though I knew what I would order. A twenty-something girl with blond streaked hair pulled back in a ponytail and wearing a brown visor with a pink DD looked up with a friendly smile.

"What would you like?"

I thought of the early days in my highchair and later when Mom made classic raised donuts in our Larimer Avenue kitchen. I'm still working through forgiving my mother for spoiling those memories. Yet, I still cling to them. And to my love for her.

I turned to the girl behind the counter. "I'll have one glazed donut, please."

"Is that it?" she asked.

"Yeah, that's enough," I said, knowing it had to be.

A sweet moment with my mom.

XIV

Driving in Cars

Mom asked me to teach her how to drive at seventy-one years old. I didn't realize she was seventy-one; like everyone else in the family, I believed her to be in her mid-sixties. Mom lied so much about her age that I'm not sure she actually knew how old she was. My mother had never driven, relying on my dad for transportation for the past twenty or so years. Before that, she depended on friends, public transportation, or walking. But in 1992, Dad had another stroke followed by a heart attack—the second of three such combined incidents—and he could no longer drive.

"Do you think I could learn?" Mom asked. "I would hate to have to sell the car and go back to asking people for rides."

"Sure," I replied. "Why not? You're healthy and alert, and you have good judgment. I can teach you."

I tried to picture Mom behind the wheel of their white Chevy Citation. She'd probably need to sit on a pillow to raise her five-foot two-inch frame, and frankly, I wasn't entirely certain she'd be a good driver. Mom epitomized what we Pittsburghers call "nebby," engrossed in what was happening around her, and I feared she might be easily distracted. But I figured that if it looked like she'd be a danger to herself or others, I could always stop the lessons.

I had taught my father to drive when he was almost fifty. At that point, my parents had never owned a car; it was a luxury they couldn't afford. When I graduated from high school in 1964, my Aunt Edith gave me five-hundred dollars to use as a down payment on a used car. I had just turned seventeen and gotten a job at Sears, so I had the money to make monthly payments, and my parents pitched in for the insurance.

I don't remember who gave us a ride, but Aunt Edith and I shopped alone at one of the used car lots lining Baum Boulevard. She knew little more than I did about cars, so we wandered through the lot staring at one vehicle after another, not knowing what to look for. A salesman approached, and after a bit of conversation about what I would use the car for and what I could afford, he led us toward a lime green 1962 Dodge Dart. It had a wide front grill and elongated fins down the sides, making it look like a smiling green dolphin. I wasn't much interested in the car's exterior, nor did I have any interest, or knowledge for that matter, in what was under the hood or how the car performed. I was more concerned with the interior.

The Dodge Dart had a vinyl bench seat with a pull-down center armrest that created faux buckets, a very cool feature for its time. Push buttons on the contoured instrument panel allowed you to select gears, and the AM radio, also with push button controls, included stereo speakers. I pictured myself behind the wheel, driving to pick up my friends, cruising through Eat n' Park on Washington Boulevard to see if we spotted any of our boy crushes. Then we'd head to Shadyside, where we'd ride down Walnut Street slowly so that we could see and be seen. Aunt Edith agreed that the Dodge Dart was a good choice, and after filling out paperwork and giving the salesman the down payment, I drove out of the lot.

While the car allowed me the freedom to go to Eat n' Park and out with my friends, owning the Dart came with some obligations. I became responsible for taking Mom grocery shopping a couple of times a week, to church each Sunday, and to her friends' houses for card club. Mom chatted on and on in the car, mostly about her friends.

"Connie's in the hospital," she said.

"I don't know Connie, Mom."

"Sure, you do," she insisted.

This is how conversations with my mother went, the minutia of a myriad of Mom's friends that I didn't know and couldn't keep up with. They weren't from the old neighborhood. I tuned Mom out, but she rambled on, seeming not to notice. Spending time in the car with Mom was a chore, and I just wanted to get her to her destination.

After a year or so of driving Mom around, I suggested to my parents that one of them learn how to drive. Mom was uncomfortable with the idea, but Dad seemed enthusiastic. I mentioned that he could take lessons from a driving school as I had, but Dad thought he could teach himself. "Just ride with me the first couple of times," he said. "I'll get the hang of it."

Dad and I got in my lime green smiling dolphin and headed toward Highland Park. I drove between the stone pillars at the end of Highland Avenue and pulled over to the side of the road that circled the reservoir. Then Dad and I got out of the car and switched places. Once in the driver's seat, I showed Dad how the push button gear selection worked and familiarized him with the pedals and turn signal. I thought about Dad and me all those years ago in Larimer schoolyard, how he placed my hands on the bike handlebars, showed me where to put my feet on the pedals, then ran behind me as I rode off to circle the schoolyard, calling out to me to be careful. I never learned how to ride a bike, and I hoped that teaching Dad to drive would be more successful.

After a few minutes of instructions, Dad said he was ready. With a determined look, eyes fixed, mouth tight, he put the car in gear and aimed it toward the road, starting, stopping, jolting, jerking, his hands gripping the wheel. He was the first to start laughing. It began as a chuckle, then we both broke into a full-out snorting horse laugh until Dad had to pull the car over. After taking a few minutes to collect ourselves, we headed out again.

Dad learned to drive after a few more trips to the park and some practice parallel parking and driving out in traffic. We shared the car, and Dad took over driving Mom to church and shopping. While I was thankful to be relieved of this responsibility, I did feel a bit sorry for Dad.

After the stroke, Dad could no longer drive, and my parents could have sold their car to eliminate the upkeep and insurance payments. Yet, Mom had come to rely on having transportation, and she didn't want to give it up. I mentally prepared for her driving lessons. A day or two after our initial conversation, I got a call from Mom.

"I've changed my mind about driving," she said.

"What do you mean? Mom, I think it's much better if one of you is able to drive. Not just for convenience, but for emergencies."

"He doesn't want me to do it," she said. I knew that by *he*, she meant Dad.

"For heaven's sake, why not?"

"He's afraid I'll leave him alone too much."

I could understand the root of Dad's fear. Mom was an active member of the Christian Mothers at Saint Raphael's Church, belonged to two card clubs, and volunteered at the community senior center. Mom easily adapted to new neighbors and neighborhoods. In her later years, Mom was treasurer of her local AARP chapter and went on occasional bus trips that they sponsored to places like Atlantic City or Lancaster, Pennsylvania. She had many friends and preferred going out rather than staying home. I can imagine her in the Chevy Citation, a few of her friends in the car, driving to Eat n' Park for a slice of their strawberry pie.

On the other hand, Dad was a homebody who favored reading Western novels, playing Scrabble with his friend John, solving crossword puzzles, or watching the Pittsburgh Pirates on television. But Dad liked having Mom at home with him, or at least nearby, either on the front porch visiting neighbors or with my Aunt Dahlia, who lived across the street. So, I wasn't surprised that he feared Mom would go out more often if she had the freedom to drive. They sold the car, and she returned to relying on friends for transportation. It was an unselfish gesture on Mom's part, but not surprising.

Before Dad's Chevy Citation went to its new owner, I removed the crucifix he had affixed to the dashboard, where it remained the entire time he owned the car. Dad's crucifix has stayed with me through my Nissan Maxima, an Acura, and two Honda CRVs. It's now resting at the bottom of my console cubicle under hand sanitizer, my library card, and lip gloss. Even out of sight, I know it's there, a part of Dad driving along with me.

Dad and I began driving in my car together some years later during one of the last summers of his life. He wasn't getting out of the house much, and Mom suggested we start taking Sunday drives to North Park to ride around the beautiful lake. I collected Mom and Dad that first Sunday, and we spent about two hours on our excursion, out Route 8 to

Wildwood Road, into the park, and then circling the lake several times. Dad sat up front with me, quiet, looking out the window, smiling. Mom sat in the back, commenting on the passing cars, the joggers around the lake, and the weather. When I arrived the following Sunday, Mom and Dad were waiting on the front porch. Dad was ready with his walker to make his way to the car as soon as I parked. Mom helped him down the few steps to the sidewalk, and I came around to open the passenger door to help him in.

"She's not going with us," Dad said.

"Why not, Mom?" I asked, turning to her.

"He said it's better with just you and him," she replied.

I searched Mom's face for signs of disappointment or hurt, but she revealed nothing. Truth be told, even though I felt bad for Mom being rejected so out of hand, I was glad to have this precious time alone with my dad. Time to sit together, in silence if we chose, in conversation if we liked. Just sharing the quiet space inside the car, side by side, our space, our time.

Dad and I drove around North Park Lake every Sunday through that summer and fall. We didn't talk much, but when we did, it was usually Dad asking questions. He was interested in the details of my life and wanted to hear about how my sons were doing in school, what I was studying, and what books I was reading. Dad, who was forced to leave school in the tenth grade to support himself, was an avid reader hungry for learning. He especially liked words, and I remember one summer when I was in elementary school, he assigned me the dictionary to read.

"Start at the beginning and go through all the words," he said. "Stop when you don't know one and read all the definitions. That's what I did."

The lesson must have stuck. In grad school, I kept a philosophy dictionary at my side while reading Aristotle and Plato. My professor recommended skipping over some of the words I didn't know, saying, "You'll never get through the program taking this much time to read." I thought it an affront to the great philosophers and continued to consult the dictionary. Dad would have approved.

Dad counted the people as we circled the lake, an obsession consistent with his increasing need for order brought on by his strokes. We listened to CDs I bought with his favorite music: Jerry Vale, Dean Martin, and the Mills Brothers. Dad was amazed that a full selection of songs could fit on a CD.

"All those songs are on this?" he asked, holding a disc up for inspection.

Sharing the car with Dad was pure joy, singing along to the Mills Brothers' "Up a Lazy River." Dad and I had this easy way of being together, synchronous, savoring our time.

In the fall, we watched the leaves turn from green to amber and purple, then saw them fall to the ground, leaving the trees barren. Dad wondered aloud if he would see the trees sprout new growth in the spring.

"Of course you will, Daddy," I reassured him. I smothered my fear of losing him, pushing the dread down to the pit of my stomach where it would fester.

We continued our rides each Sunday except for those days in the dead of winter when it was too cold for Dad to go out or too snowy for me to drive. One Sunday early the following spring, after we had resumed our drives, Dad remarked that he could see buds on the trees.

"Look at that," he said, pointing out the window to a Maple tree. He sounded surprised, pleased. I felt optimistic.

As we circled the lake, Dad counted the joggers and dog walkers. We rode together to North Park each Sunday until June when Dad had his final stroke and heart attack.

I hadn't been back to North Park for years until I cut through the park on a recent Saturday afternoon on my way to a shopping mall in the North Hills. On impulse, I turned off the main road toward the lake. It was the kind of spring day that shook off winter and almost demanded our presence outside. Joggers and dog walkers populated the path, young couples strolled hand-in-hand, and children darted up and down the grass slope between the path and the lake's edge. I opened the sunroof, inviting in the warmth and glancing at the passing trees.

On my second circle around the lake, I spotted a girl of about six or seven riding a two-wheel bike. She struggled to keep the bike upright, her legs peddling as fast as she could. Then, I noticed the young man—presumably her dad—running behind her. I smiled and wondered if she knew how lucky she was.

XV

Mim

I opened an email from Sean with a link to a Zillow site and the message "Check this out." Sean was looking for a townhouse or duplex for himself and Alex as they were growing out of their two-bedroom apartment. Pleased that he seemed to be asking for my opinion, I clicked on the link. It opened to a photo of a familiar address—Mim's last apartment. I scanned the images: remodeled kitchen, new hardwood floors, and new carpeting in the dining room, which had been converted to a second bedroom. I came to the photo of Mim and Uncle's bedroom and returned to the last time I stood in that room twenty years earlier.

A normal Saturday, I'd given myself permission to stay in bed until eight, made a pot of coffee, then hit the treadmill. After my run, I ate my usual bowl of granola with berries, drank two cups of strong black coffee, and enjoyed a long hot shower. I was drying off when the call came from Mom.

"I can't reach Mim."

Mim and Uncle had continued as my second parents from the earliest days in our Larimer Avenue apartment through my teens and adulthood. Uncle provided transportation whenever I needed it and inspired my love of gardening. Mim took me shopping for back-to-school shoes, gave me my weekly allowance (likely proceeds from her gambling), and listened to my dramatic accounts of high school crushes.

I was in my early forties when Uncle had a heart attack. Mim spent the days that followed in Uncle's room at Shadyside Hospital, feeding him homemade chicken pastina soup, making sure he had a fresh blanket, and keeping his spirits up with games of poker.

At about 11:00 one night, Mim called me from the hospital. "You have to come now," she said. I arrived moments too late and found Mim standing beside Uncle's bed, cradling his hand in hers and looking up at me with eyes that said, "I needed you."

Uncle's face was without color, his hazel eyes open, seeming to stare off at something distant, perhaps something miraculous. Mim caressed his forehead, closing his eyes. I stood across from her and reached for Uncle's other hand. Neither of us cried. We were numb.

After the funeral service, Uncle's cremated remains were placed in a simple urn inside a cardboard box that Mim tenderly rested on a shelf in her bedroom closet. "He likes it there," she insisted.

Mim's sparkle faded after Uncle was gone. Her walk slowed, and her laugh became vacant, losing its joy. She shared quiet visits with my mom and dad while her friends went to play Bingo or cards. I yearned for the old Mim, quick to laugh, spilling over with energy and excitement. It crushed me to see her diminished, moderated, aged.

We moved our traditional Christmas Eve dinner from Mim's house to mine. She gave me her pizzelle maker saying, "You'll use it more than I will now." She also informed me that I was executrix of her will, a notion simultaneously horrifying and comical. There was no estate beyond the plastic-covered furniture and the decorative cherubs that hung from mirrors and lamps. Of course, there was her 1950s Universal-Cribben five burner, double oven gas range that Sean used until 2016.

"Have the family come and take whatever they want—you and your mother first," Mim said. "I have insurance, so you won't have to worry about funeral expenses."

When I found her on her bedroom floor that Saturday morning, Mim wore a pink and yellow print nightgown, her glasses sat on the nightstand, and the television was on with the volume turned up. Her familiar gold chain with the Blessed Mother medal lay distorted to one side on her neck. Her eyes were closed, but her mouth remained slightly open as if she wanted to say something. Did she call out for help? Did she utter a prayer? Kneeling close beside her between the twin beds, I reached for her hand. It was cold and surprisingly hard. How long had she been here alone on the floor? I shuddered and stood. The television blared, and I reached to turn it off. Sitting on the side of Mim's unmade bed, I studied her face, trying to process what I was seeing, feeling. I didn't cry just then—that came days later in storms of wailing—but I felt sick to my stomach like I might vomit. I took deep breaths and swallowed hard.

Thinking back, I wished I had spoken to Mim, said, "I love you," and told her how she was the spark of delight that punctuated my life. But I don't remember saying anything. I'm guessing, hoping, that she knew all that I didn't say.

I called 911 from Mim's kitchen wall phone, returned to her side, and waited. I'm not sure how long I sat there before the paramedics arrived. I watched from the doorway as they did a cursory examination, presumably to be certain she was dead. They removed her jewelry—the gold chain, her wedding ring—and handed it to me. Then they lifted her, laid her on a stretcher, and slid Mim into a maroon-colored vinyl bag. *No. Don't zip it up. Please don't treat her like baggage.* I swallowed the bile that rose to my throat.

They carried Mim down the steps while I followed behind. "Be careful turning her on the landing," I cautioned. Out on the street, the paramedics glided Mim into the back of an ambulance, then closed and latched the double doors. I watched, hugging myself against the February chill, as they disappeared down Collins Avenue.

Back upstairs, I looked around, mind muddled as I tried to figure out what to do next. I went into the bedroom and opened the closet door. I studied the humble cardboard box on the shelf and felt some relief that Mim didn't die alone after all. I gently lifted the box from what had been its home for the past two years.

"You'll stay with me, Uncle, until it's time for your resting place together," I said aloud. I held him close as I closed the apartment and walked down to the street.

I don't know how long I stared at the Zillow photo of Mim's bedroom, thinking back to the details of that day, before it occurred to me that my mom had been there with me. She got a ride from a neighbor and met me at Mim's apartment with the key. I ran up the steps ahead to find Mim's body. I was kneeling beside her when Mom reached the bedroom door and saw her sister on the floor. She screamed, stomping her foot repeatedly on the worn carpet. I can still hear her scream. How could I have forgotten that Mom was there?

I held Mom as I reached behind her to turn off the television. I walked her into the living room to sit and brought her a glass of water from the kitchen. Mom sat on the sofa while I called 911, while I waited with Mim for the paramedics, while they zipped Mim into the vinyl bag, carried her down to the ambulance, and drove away. After I returned upstairs and retrieved Uncle's remains from the bedroom closet, I helped Mom from the sofa, and we walked down the stairs together, me holding on to her, carrying Uncle in my other arm.

How did all of this vanish from my earlier recollection? It's funny how memory works, faulty and unreliable. Without realizing it, we select, revise, put some details into focus, and lose others. We recreate our version of the past through our own lens. I wonder why I chose to initially delete Mom from this intense memory. Perhaps I wanted the intimacy of those final moments with Mim to be mine alone, to cherish the uncluttered privacy of this final shared experience with my other mother.

XVI

My Father's Hands

I wheeled my father from his room down the carpeted hallway of the Squirrel Hill Rehabilitation Center toward the elevators. I noticed that pushing his wheelchair felt effortless, almost weightless. I looked down at his full head of silver-white hair. "He's the only male patient that needs a blow dryer after his shower," his nurse liked to say. We entered the large elevator and rode down to the first floor. When the wide silver doors opened, we exited from the side of the building to a small square concrete patio with metal tables and chairs that faced Wilkins Avenue. The July air smelled almost spring-like, and the warm sun comforted my face. Dad put his frail hand into the bag of breadcrumbs I had brought from home and tossed several pieces on the ground in front of him. He watched with amusement as the birds fed.

"Look at that little fella," he said, laughing. "The little one got the breadcrumb."

We stayed outside for a short while, and then Dad said he was tired. "I think that's enough for today, babe." I wheeled Dad back to his room and pushed the call button for the nurse to help me lift him into bed. My father was gaunt and weak, his frame a diminutive version of his former self. I was doing what I imagine many adult children do every day, watching a parent shrink with age and illness, sitting exhausted and afraid at a hospital bedside, cradling a hand that once held our own.

Dad was strong as a younger man, so strong that he could lift me on his shoulders, could carry me anywhere—could carry anything anywhere, it seemed. I thought about my small hand enfolded in Dad's walking across the Larimer Avenue Bridge, singing "On the Sunny Side of the Street." I remembered him steadying me on my first two-wheel bike and holding me atop the garden railing at Mellon Park so I could see the green hillside below, a tree spotted vast expanse of grass overlooking Fifth Avenue.

Dad's boney fingers reached for the box of Kleenex and moved it to the right just an inch. Everything on his bedside table—glasses, pad, pen, deck of cards—had to be in their assigned spots. I chuckled to myself at his obsessive organization, knowing that I've inherited more than a bit of it, compulsively organizing my underwear drawer by color, moving picture frames just an inch or so to their original place after my cleaning lady leaves.

I reached for the deck of cards. "What should we play today?" I asked. Dad liked double solitaire and kings, and I liked gin rummy.

"How about gin rummy?" he suggested, reaching for his glasses.

I smiled and dealt ten cards each. Dad gathered his cards in skeletal hands, covered with pale, almost sheer skin. I studied his fingers, long and graceful, knuckles deeply furrowed, revealing years of tightening and opening, wafer-thin ridged nails neatly trimmed. I thought about the time years earlier when Dad came home from work one day, his right hand swollen the size of a small melon. He had broken his hand punching the side of a park maintenance truck, explaining later to Mom that it was either the truck or his co-worker. Mom insisted that he go to the emergency room, but Dad refused, resting quietly at the kitchen table, his hand immersed in Mom's large pasta pot filled with ice cubes. I remember being amazed that he could withstand the pain without even a wince. When did his hands become so flimsy, so insubstantial?

We played a few hands of gin rummy, with Dad keeping score. He won most games and chastised me repeatedly for not remembering which cards were already thrown. Dad was still competitive as always, just like when I was little and he wouldn't let me win at checkers or chess until I could win on my own merit. The tragic contrast between his keen mind and fragile body seemed somehow a betrayal, and I felt powerless to make it right.

On a visit late one Saturday afternoon, I found Dad sitting in his wheelchair alone. His small but cheerful private room had a large window that overlooked Wilkins Avenue, and I was glad that he had a view of passing cars and people, of the Linden trees that lined the street, of birds that perched in the trees and sometimes settled on his windowsill. Dad wore blue-striped cotton pajamas and brown backless slippers Mom brought from home. I hated those slippers. I feared he'd fall, and I made a mental note to pick up a pair with backs. Dad stared at his hands in his lap, and he didn't look up when I entered the room.

"Hi, Daddy," I said with as much cheer as I could muster. He didn't respond. As I got closer, I saw that he was crying, something he did more often with each stroke.

"What's wrong, Daddy?"

"I'm going to die here," he said. "I'm going to die in this place. You have to get me out of here."

"Well, where do you want to go?"

"Home," he said, amazed that it wasn't obvious to me.

"Of course," I said.

That evening, I called Mom and talked about moving Dad home. "He said the same thing when I was there earlier today," she said. "What do you think? Do you think he can do all right at home?"

"I have no idea, Mom. I'll meet with his nurse and physical therapist tomorrow."

The next day, Mom and I discussed the possibility of Dad's release with his doctor, nurse, and therapist. They were pessimistic. He hadn't recovered from his stroke and still needed rehabilitation, although most days, he was too frail to make much progress and spent most of his time in bed or his wheelchair. I suggested arranging for rehab at home for a while, or I could bring him in for outpatient rehab. His doctor didn't think it was the best solution but agreed that we could give it a try.

Dad lasted two days at home. He was too weak to get in and out of bed without help. He couldn't go to the bathroom or bathe alone. Mom became his nurse, washing his thick silver hair, applying lotion to his feet, and dressing him in fresh pajamas. On the second day home, I got a call from Mom.

"He wanted to go downstairs to have breakfast in the dining room," she said. "I tried to talk him out of it, but he was insistent, so I gave in."

Mom attempted to help him down the stairs, but she didn't have the strength to support him. Dad tripped and fell a couple of steps. They sat together on the stairs of their little townhouse and cried.

"He has to go back," she said. "We can't do it."

Dad's primary doctor and his physical therapist hadn't seen much progress in Dad's rehabilitation, and he didn't go back to the rehab center. Instead, he was admitted to Heritage House, a nursing facility. His semi-private room, shared with an eighty-year-old man with heart failure, was sterile and felt more like a hospital than the cheerful room at the rehab center. He spent most of the day in bed. The staff allowed him to decide if he wanted to participate in rehab. He didn't. Dad stopped asking to go home and seemed resigned to his situation. I resisted, telling myself that Dad would get stronger. This can't be the end, I told myself. I'm not ready, even if he is.

After a couple of weeks, Dad refused to eat solid food. I visited him daily at dinnertime and encouraged him to eat. "Check out this soup, Daddy. Probably not as good as Mom's, but it looks tasty." He refused, but I persisted—two stubborn minds at cross purposes.

I thought of all the times Dad and I had planted our feet on opposing sides, arguments over the length of my skirt, and disagreements over my weekend curfew. When I wanted to drive at age sixteen, Dad said, "I don't care what the Commonwealth of Pennsylvania says; you're not driving until you're seventeen." With a lifetime of experience in being obstinate, Dad prevailed.

Soon after he decided to stop eating, the nurses began bringing a can of Boost to his room a few times a day. Dad refused to drink it, and we continued to argue. *Damn it, Daddy*, I thought. *How can you just give up?*

I thought about sitting at the kitchen table with my dad when I was eight, waiting for my mom to serve dinner. She had set my plate in front of me and said, "It's flank steak," but I immediately recognized the greyish, foul-smelling piece of meat as liver.

"It's not steak. It's liver. I know it's liver."

"Well, you have to eat it," Mom said.

"Linda, do you like liver?" Dad asked.

"I hate it, Daddy. I really hate it."

"Then you don't have to eat it," he said.

Mom insisted that a child eat whatever is in front of them.

"Not if they don't like it," Dad said. "No one should be forced to eat what they don't want, even a child."

Relieved, I ate the potatoes and green beans and left the liver untouched.

Days in the nursing facility dragged on. Dad took in only water, but we stopped arguing about it. He got weaker. We stopped playing cards. He talked less, so it was up to me to sustain our communication. I told him about books I was reading and what I studied in grad school. He liked hearing about my garden and how I was still harvesting huge zucchini in late September. Our conversations reminded me of our talks the previous summer while riding around North Park Lake. Dad's eyes brightened each time I entered his room. It became difficult for me to leave each evening. Would this be the last night?

It was early October. Soon, the air would become crisp, then cold. Leaves would turn yellow and orange and drop from their branches, twirling in a death spiral to the ground. Dad seemed vacant. We still made eye connections, and he used hand signals to ask for a glass of water or to raise his bed. Dad took some pleasure, though, in watching the Pirate games on television. That's what he was doing the last time I saw him when I waved and said, "See you later, Daddy," and watched him lift his fragile hand to wave back.

PART THREE

Bequeathing the Legacy

*"Tradition is not the worship of ashes,
but the preservation of fire."*
—Gustav Mahler

XVII

Three Fishes and a Ham

A few weeks before Christmas of 2019, Jason stopped by. "Mom, I have something to ask you," he said. I wondered what he was setting me up for. "Is it okay if I bring a ham for Christmas Eve dinner?"

The voice in my head screamed, *No! How could you even suggest such a thing?* I wondered if Jason knew what he was asking, how deeply I felt rooted in these traditions, what value I had placed in each custom, each ritual, and how painful it was to let go.

***

A photo of Mom and Dad appeared in the *Pittsburgh Sun-Telegraph,* our local newspaper: Dad looking straight into the camera and Mom kissing him on the cheek. It was the fall of 1954, and Dad had won $250 in a football contest sponsored by the paper. The photo and accompanying brief article made my parents neighborhood celebrities, and Mom was giddy with excitement, sharing the clipping with Mim and neighbors. The newspaper quoted Dad saying that part of the winnings would go for a transformer for his daughter Linda's electric train: "I've been promising her for two years that I would get a new one, and now I can." The article said Dad also planned to buy "a new coat and a desk that the seven-year-old has been asking for." I don't recall if I got the coat or the desk, but I remember getting the transformer.

The train was the most important piece of our Christmas tree for Dad and me. Mom and Dad split up the tree decorating, with Mom in charge of hanging colored glass ornaments and tinsel and Dad responsible for creating a little town below the tree. Dad said that he'd always wanted a real tree that gave off a pine smell, but we put up the same artificial tree each year because Mom said that she didn't want the dirt of a real one. "There will be needles making a mess everywhere." Our tree stood about three feet tall with sparse, thin branches that looked like dyed green toilet brushes.

My childhood artificial tree sat on an end table in a corner of the living room. Dad placed a piece of plywood on top of the table to increase the surface; then, he positioned the skimpy tree in the center and covered the table with a sheet before constructing the village. He stacked books under one end of the sheet to create a hillside to which he added little plastic replicas of pine trees and miniature metal skiers with tiny skis and poles. I got to sprinkle fake snow made of asbestos over everything. I watched his hands spread ground coffee to form narrow roads around the flat part of the surface below the hillside, then add the train tracks on the outer edge. Dad and I knelt before the tree as though we were worshiping something celestial.

I'm not sure from where or how, but Dad had accumulated pieces of a Lionel train set that included a black engine, a milk truck with a rounded silver container, and a couple of orange box cars. We had a small black transformer with a switch and a few dials, but it never worked, so we moved the train cars by hand. Once we got the new transformer, a square black box with two handles—one orange for direction and one black for speed—the electric train could run on its own. Dad showed me how to operate it, and he bought me a small red plastic whistle that I used to warn our little village that the train was coming. Dad smiled in approval.

Once the train was set up, Dad and I populated our little town: a white plastic barn with a slanted red roof, a couple of brown plastic horses, and several tiny metal figures—a milkman carrying bottles, a girl in a red cloak with white lining, a train conductor with a blue cap. Finally, Dad created a little park off to one side with more miniature trees and a green plastic park bench. He added a small square mirror upon which I had the honor of placing the tiny metal figure of an ice skater with yellow hair and white skates dressed in a red circle skirt. Dad took extreme care so the moving train didn't disrupt the buildings and figures. The whole thing was magical. And it was ours—Dad's and mine.

It wasn't until I left home at age twenty-one that I finally had a live tree. Dad came with me to buy it from his friend, Nick, who sold trees out of a vacant lot across the street from Morningside School in the neighborhood where my parents had settled. Nick held up one tree at a time while Dad and I walked around each, inspecting, then dismissing them as not tall enough or full enough. About the fourth try, Nick held a six-foot pine with lush branches and a thick trunk. Dad and I put our noses into the boughs to take in the strong scent. We agreed that this was the one. Nick and Dad bound the tree with rope and tied it to the top of my car. I carefully drove the few miles to my place, and once there, I held the doors open while Dad carried the tree to my second-floor apartment. He shaved the thick trunk to fit in the stand and made a wooden frame, attaching the stand to it with large screws to create a sturdy base. Once the tree was secure, Dad and I rubbed the branches between our palms, then held our hands to our noses, savoring the pine aroma. Dad grinned. "Now, that's a Christmas tree," he said.

I enjoyed live Christmas trees for another forty years, returning each year to Nick's lot and using the stand and frame that Dad built. At some point, I switched from pine to a white fir variety that smelled like citrus. But struggling with a live tree seemed to get more difficult each year, especially after my husband died, and I had to rely on my sons to drive with me to pick up the tree, carry it home, and set it up. In 2016, a friend convinced me to buy an artificial tree. It was an expensive option from a company called Balsam Hill that promised the tree would look real. It does look authentic, but even though Dad died many years before, I feel like a traitor putting it up each year.

As a child, we spent Christmas Eve at Grandma's house. I loved gathering around the porcelain-topped kitchen table with my cousins and the banging of the back screen door each time someone came in or went out to the backyard. I loved Baw Baw calling to me in his thick Italian, "*Leenda, vieni qui*," and my aunts and uncles' voices spilling in from the dining room, where we played card games, sang songs, and shared meals that lasted so long that we needed intermission between courses.

While a few aunts, uncles, and cousins often came to Grandma's for Sunday dinners, most of my mom's extended family showed up for holidays. On Easter Sunday, we gathered for lunch after Mass when Grandma served homemade cavatelli and her Easter salad with sliced oranges, salami, and green olives, which was one of my favorites. On Thanksgiving, we sat for hours eating two dinners, first the Italian one with ravioli and meatballs and then the classic American dinner with turkey and trimmings.

Christmas Eve was the Feast of the Seven Fishes, a celebration that immigrants from Southern Italy (like most of us in our Larimer Avenue neighborhood) carried with them to their new home. The feast is rooted in the Catholic tradition of abstaining from eating meat the day before Christmas. Various theories attempt to explain the reason for the number seven, but Mom told me that it represents the seven sacraments. Grandma's version of the feast began with spaghetti with anchovies and garlic, then proceeded with stuffed calamari, salted cod that Italians call *baccala*, fried smelts with their heads still attached, shrimp sautéed in lots of garlic and parsley, and other seafood that rotated from year to year. One year, Uncle arrived with a bulky package that he laid on Grandma's kitchen table. As he unwrapped the white butcher paper, my cousins and I crowded around, anxious to see what might be inside. Uncle pulled back the wrapping to reveal an eel, a huge brownish-black snake-like fish, which sent us kids screaming and running from Grandma's kitchen.

After Christmas Eve dinner, Uncle Richard, my mom's youngest brother, entertained us kids by teaching us to juggle using oranges from Grandma's fruit bowl. I was never very good at it, but my cousin Tommy caught on right away, and the rest of us cousins clapped and cheered. Mim organized a game of penny poker, sitting at the end of the dining room table with a coffee can filled with pennies, making change. "Who's in?" she called into the kitchen. We kids were allowed to play for a while, but soon the adults took over and raised the stakes. One of Grandma's opera records played on the old phonograph in the background, competing with the chatter from the card game.

My cousins and I had a mini sleepover on Christmas Eve; we were sent to one of the second-floor bedrooms and got into our pajamas when it got late. I crammed into the only bed with my cousins Danielle and Jackie, sisters around my age. Tommy lay in a heap of folded blankets on the floor. We waited for Santa. I tried to fall asleep, but Danielle and Jackie fought over the covers and the placement of their limbs, and Tommy made thumping noises on the floor to fool us into believing it was Santa on Grandma's roof. Eventually, we'd fall asleep until our parents woke us when it was time to leave. Mom would put my coat on over my pajamas, and Dad carried me the two blocks home.

When I was about twelve, Mim took over our Christmas Eve fish dinner. Grandma had moved to California to be with Aunt Gilda, where the milder weather was easier for her arthritis. My parents and sisters, Mim and Uncle, Aunt Jo and Tommy crowded around Mim's dining room table in her small apartment. Mim served just five fishes: spaghetti with anchovies, shrimp, calamari, *baccala*, and smelts. After dinner, she put out trays of homemade pizzelles, dried figs, and Torrone candy to enjoy while we played penny ante poker. It wasn't the same as Grandma's dinners with all the aunts, uncles, and cousins, but the most important people in my life were there.

Mim continued to host Christmas Eve, and as a young adult, I began the tradition of shopping with her in the Strip District to prepare for our feast. A literal strip of land about a mile long, this is where you could buy food from the old country in stores run by Italian immigrants. Imported olive oil and hot peppers at Jimmy and Nino Sunseri's, Italian cheeses and fresh pasta at Pennsylvania Macaroni, or what we called Penn Mac, and cured meats at Parma Sausage. The Strip was one of those places that reminded me of who I am and where I came from. It felt like the old neighborhood.

I parked my car on one of the side streets where I could get a spot, and Mim and I made our way onto crowded Penn Avenue like marchers taking our place in a parade, picking up the rhythm of the shoppers. Our first stop was Wholey's to buy fish and seafood, the staples of our dinner. We headed for the salmon, an addition to our menu in place of *baccala* that almost no one still ate. Mim asked a patient young man behind the counter to hold up one salmon filet after another until she was satisfied.

"No, that one's too small. How about the one behind it? No, not that one—the other one." It reminded me of Dad and I selecting a Christmas tree. I saved a spot in the long line at the shrimp counter while Mim went to get calamari and smelts. "It's okay to get frozen calamari," she explained later, "It's pre-cleaned and less work." Then we were off to Penn Mac for fresh linguini and a stop at Ursula's cheese counter for some asiago for snacking and parmesan for grating.

Our last stop was Sunseri's, where a teenage girl stood near the door playing Christmas carols and Italian folk songs on her accordion—a little "Jingle Bells" and a bit of "Santa Lucia." Jimmy Sunseri, an unlit cigar protruding from the side of his mouth, called hello to Mim as he dipped a large spoon into a stainless-steel container of peppers and onions. We weaved through the narrow aisles, and Mim stopped to scoop cured black olives from a wooden bin.

"Always get the olives here soaking in brine, not the ones in the case," she said. Mim reached for a loaf of crusty Italian bread while I stretched for a box of Torrone candy from a high shelf.

I was never a fan of the taste of Torrone, a nougat and toasted almond confection, but I loved the packaging. La Florentine brand came in a cream-colored box with a portrait of an exquisite-looking Renaissance lady on the front. Inside, the individual candies were packaged in decorated rectangular boxes. When we were little, Tommy and I would stack the small boxes to create towers, bridges, and buildings. Then we took out the candy and removed the thin flakey coating from each side. We pretended to offer each other communion, taking turns placing the wafer-like film on each other's tongues and making the sign of the cross.

Mim and I made our last purchase of the day from Sunseri's bakery section—two *sfogliatelle*. The layered pastry filled with custard became a ritual. When we finished shopping and returned to Mim's, we'd put the groceries away and sit at her dining room table with coffee and our *sfogliatelle*.

I took over Christmas Eve after Mim died. Uncle and my parents are gone now too. I go to the Strip alone, retracing our steps, Wholey's, Penn Mac, Sunseri's. Jimmy Sunseri doesn't seem to remember me, but he always returns my smile. There's comfort in the Strip. While more tourists populate the streets and stores than in the old days, and many outdoor stands sell Steelers hats and scarves instead of biscotti, there are still enough reminders to make it feel like home. The girl—now a young woman—with the accordion still greets shoppers in front of Sunseri's, and the strong aroma of coffee continues to spill from Fortuna's shop. I finish my shopping with one *sfogliatelle* to eat when I get home. Then, I walk along the main street, spending time among those to whom I belong.

I make just three fish now, starting with linguini and fresh clams instead of anchovies—I never liked their salty taste—followed by sauteed shrimp and baked salmon, the dishes my sons eat. I used to make calamari, but it became too much work as our family got smaller, and I noticed that I was the only one eating it, so it went the way of the *baccala*. I serve the shrimp on a platter that belonged to my mom, and I use Mim's small cut glass bowl for grated parmesan. I pour water into Grandma's gold-trimmed etched glasses. I read somewhere that the children of my generation often see family heirlooms as a burden and end up selling their parents' treasures in a yard sale, or worse, just tossing them out. I look at these cherished fragments of the past and worry that Sean and Jason might view them as just old stuff.

My sister moved to Maryland a while back, and she and her husband return to Pittsburgh for Christmas only every other year. My sons are single now, so I sometimes set the table for only three of us. I use Mim's recipe to make pizzelles and put them on the table after dinner. The pizzelles are labor intensive as the iron only makes two at a time. While the iron is preheating, I blend the sugar and butter, then add the remaining ingredients: flour, eggs, baking powder, vanilla, and anise. I don't use my KitchenAid food processor, preferring to mix the ingredients by hand the way Mim taught me. I spoon just the right amount of batter onto each of the two snowflake motifs on the pizzelle iron, then count to fifty. I gently remove the pizzelles with a fork and place them on the tea towels that line my kitchen counter. I memorialize the old days. I know I'm trying to keep them alive by holding on to their food and traditions.

One evening after a holiday dinner, my sons and I cleared the table, and Sean came into the dining room to find me sitting alone, crying.

It was the year my mother died, the last of her generation. Sean sat in the chair beside me. "It doesn't matter how long you sit here, Mom," he said, touching my shoulder. "They're not coming back." More truth than poetry from my firstborn son.

When Jason asked about bringing a ham for Christmas Eve dinner, I realized this was the beginning of dismantling a long line of traditions. Yet, I took a deep breath and heard myself say, "Sure, it's okay." I knew it was time to grant my sons their own ways of doing things. They had been patient with my need to hang on to the old. Still, it felt like losing Grandma and Mim all over again. Who will remember after I'm gone, now that we're down to three fishes and a ham?

Each year when the boys were young, I bought Christmas ornaments for their stockings—small stuffed teddy bears, miniature ice skates, and, one year, little picture frames holding photos of them with my parents. After my sons left home, I continued to use their ornaments on my tree.

When Sean was in his thirties, he bought a house in Morningside, the neighborhood where my parents had lived for many years. It had a wide front porch and a backyard where Sean planted tomatoes, peppers, and herbs like basil and Italian parsley. The living room faced the front of the house and offered the perfect spot for a Christmas tree in front of the window. After Alex was born, Sean started putting up a live tree he bought from Nick's lot, now run by Nick's son and grandson.

I don't make stockings for my grown sons anymore, but lately, I've begun to wrap their childhood ornaments to give them as gifts. Jason asked me to hold his, but Sean seemed glad to have the ornaments for his tree. I also started giving Alex an ornament each year in her stocking—a silver letter A, a pink unicorn, and a tiny stuffed dog. When Alex was three, Sean hosted dinner on Christmas day for Jason and me. I asked if there was anything I could bring.

"Is there any leftover linguini with clams?" he asked.

"Sure. I made extra, so there's plenty."

So, he wanted the linguine and clams, I thought. I smiled as I spooned what was left of the pasta and clams into a large Tupperware container. Then, as an afterthought, I put some pizzelles into a box to take along.

I arrived at Sean's and carried the pasta and cookies into the kitchen, where he and Jason prepared a romaine salad and an antipasto of provolone cheese, pepperoni, and black olives. Jason reached for a pizzelle and gave me a hug.

"Oh, I'm glad you brought cookies," Sean said. "Thanks, Mom."

I hung up my coat and reached for Alex, who grabbed my legs.

"Come with me, Nonna. Come see my tree."

Alex took my hand and led me into the living room. We stood before the six-foot pine, and I spotted some of Sean's old ornaments hanging from branches. The picture frame with a photo of Sean and my dad held a prominent spot. Then, I looked below the tree and saw the train. My breath caught in my throat.

Sean came in from the kitchen, and Alex ran to him.

"Daddy, make the train go."

"You know how to do it," Sean said.

He sat on the floor next to Alex, took her small hand, and reached for the transformer switch. The train made its way around the tree, and Alex clapped and squealed. Sean sat back and watched her, smiling.

I sat next to Sean. "Did you know that Pops set up a train like this for me when I was little?" I told him about the train, the little village, and the skiers. Jason came from the kitchen, plugged in the tree lights, and joined us on the floor. The three of us talked, watching Alex, who was fascinated with her train.

XVIII

A Sign

Alex and I were decorating my front porch for Halloween—a haystack in the corner covered with gourds and dried Indian corn, two large pumpkins on either side of the front door, scarecrows stuck into the ground with bamboo stakes at the bottom of the porch steps. We were hanging an ominous-looking witch on the front door when Alex asked, "Nonna, do you believe in ghosts?"

I wasn't sure how to answer.

I thought about Halloween, the night when the world of the living and that of the dead supposedly came together. In the Middle Ages, the holiday was known as All Hallows Eve, the night before the Catholic celebration of All Saints' Day, created to honor the church's dead martyrs and saints. The church later added All Souls' Day the following day to commemorate Catholics who made it into heaven, who the church referred to as the faithful departed, creating a trilogy of days when Catholics like my mother honored their belief in the strong bond between the living and the dead.

I didn't believe in spirits or other supernatural manifestations. I've always been the practical type, rooted in the here and now of the physical world. I looked for logical explanations of events and dismissed those who believed in the paranormal as absurd.

So imagine how surprised I was to receive a sign from my dead father.

My awareness of supernatural signs began when my Uncle Howard, my mother's oldest brother, died in January of 1957 when I was nine. He was the first of my mother's nine siblings to pass away. According to his death certificate, it was a sudden heart attack—a coronary occlusion. He was forty-four and left behind his wife, Rose, and seven children.

The day after Uncle Howard's death, I sat beside my grandmother on one of the hard, wooden chairs in DeRosa's Funeral Home. My mom and aunts stood near the door, receiving visitors. Old women dressed in black, sitting close to each other like a coven, said the rosary in unison; some wore blessed mother medals, or charms to ward off the evil eye dangling from gold chains. I stared down at the floral carpet to not look at the satin-lined casket holding my uncle and because I couldn't look at my grandmother's heartbroken face.

"It's not God's way," Grandma said, breaking our silence. "A mother should never live to see her child dead."

I held her soft wrinkled hand in mine and hoped that it helped.

The days that followed were filled with long hours sitting at DeRosa's breathing in the aroma of flowers and listening to the buzz of conversation, evenings overflowing with family and friends at Grandma's house on Whittier Street, and finally standing shivering in the blustery cold on a hillside at Mount Carmel Cemetery. At some point, I remember hearing Mom and Mim somehow relating Uncle Howard's death to the painting of the Last Supper that hung over the buffet in my grandmother's dining room.

The story goes that the painting fell in the middle of the night, causing a loud noise as it crashed onto the buffet below. When Grandma went downstairs to see what caused the racket, she found the undamaged painting securely in its wooden frame lying on top of the buffet, having broken a set of small espresso cups on display. The nail that held the painting was still in the wall. Grandma examined the wire on the back of the frame. It remained intact. There was no apparent explanation for how the painting came off the wall. Later that morning, Grandma got the phone call that her son Howard had died at 2:10 A.M. Grandma hadn't noted when the painting fell, but she and most others in the family attributed the crash of the Last Supper painting as a sign of Howard's death.

Two years later, in February of 1959, Grandma's Last Supper painting fell again. On a Monday afternoon, Grandma was in her basement doing laundry when she heard the crash. She later said that she knew what the noise was and what it meant as soon as she heard it. Again, the undamaged Last Supper painting landed on the buffet. Again, the nail remained intact in the wall, and the wire behind the wooden frame was undisturbed. Within the hour, Grandma got a call that her son-in-law, my Uncle Anthony, had died suddenly while playing handball at the YMCA with Pittsburgh Pirates pitcher Bob Friend. It was a coronary occlusion. At fifty-three years old, he left behind my inconsolable Aunt Edith. For the family, this event sealed the connection between the dramatic fall of the painting and a family member's death.

"It was a sign," they said, nodding in agreement.

I was skeptical of the significance that my mother and Mim placed on the crash of the painting. They seemed confident in the connection. But, even as a child, I couldn't make sense of what seemed so illogical. I saw these incidents as mere coincidence and dismissed my family members as superstitious.

* * *

In 1999, my father was in the Squirrel Hill Rehabilitation Center after his third, and what turned out to be the final, stroke. I visited him daily, trying to keep him positive, engaged in conversation, and motivated for rehab. Dad occasionally spoke of the reality we both acknowledged—he would likely die soon. He asked me to help him fill out his advance directive and named me the decision-maker regarding end-of-life care. I didn't welcome this responsibility, but Dad hadn't asked for my consent. "Put your name there," he said, pointing to a line on the form that asked for the person who could legally make his health care decisions. Neither did he ask for my opinion when he gave the "Do Not Resuscitate" order. I just noticed the plastic DNR bracelet on his thin wrist one day.

Dad occasionally wondered aloud what it would feel like when he died, if he would be aware of the experience, and perhaps most important to him, if he would see his mother. Dad didn't have many shared experiences to reflect on or stories to tell about his mother since she died when he was only two years old. Now that he approached the end of his own life, he began speaking of his mother more often and expressed a longing to see her. Uncomfortable with the discussion of death and terrified to confront the reality of losing Dad, I tried to steer our conversations toward more pleasant topics like Pirates baseball, whatever Western novel he was reading, or the eggplant parmigiana that Mom brought in for his dinner.

Late one summer afternoon, we were sitting quietly, Dad working on one of his much-loved crossword puzzles and me reading an outdated magazine I found in the visitor's lounge, when I brought up the subject of death.

"Daddy, after you die, can you send me some sign that you're okay?"

My father looked up from his puzzle and stared at me for a moment, his hazel eyes narrowing. Then, he broke into a hearty laugh. "I can't do that, babe," he said. "You'd be way too scared."

"No, I wouldn't, Daddy. I could never be afraid of you." Dad kept laughing at the thought of me receiving eerie communication from beyond. I asked again, "Please, Daddy. It would mean so much to me."

"Okay, babe. If you insist." The matter settled, Dad returned to his puzzle, and I went back to the magazine. I didn't think much about his promise again for some time. My father died on a Wednesday evening, October 6, 1999. It wasn't sudden or dramatic. It was quiet, peaceful, and heartbreaking.

About six weeks after Dad's death, I had just returned home from shopping and went upstairs to change clothes when something strange happened. When I got to the top of the steps, my eyes fell on the small silver framed photo of my grandmother that sat on an antique library table in the second-floor hall. Rose was the grandmother I never knew—my father's mother, who died when he was so young. Rose, black hair pulled back in a knot at the nape of her neck, full lips formed in a half smile, perfectly arched eyebrows, and an expression that said, "I'm confident with the woman I am." I always liked that photo. Maybe because I was told I looked like her, especially our eyes. Or maybe because she was the mother of someone I adored.

I noticed the picture of Rose was tilted in its frame so that the photo appeared diagonally inside the pale pink matting. Perhaps the photo slipped and skewed when I was dusting, but I thought it strange. I opened the back of the frame, righted the picture, and then re-secured the frame backing. I paused to look into Rose's dark eyes. I was thinking about how young she looked when I felt a powerful connection with my dad. I didn't see or hear anything, yet it was more than the mere thought of him. I actually *felt* his physical presence. I stood still for a few moments holding the picture frame, staring into my grandmother's eyes, and savoring the sensation that my father was near. The feeling passed, and I returned the frame to its place on the hall table.

I held the incident close to myself for the night, but the next day, I shared it in a phone call with my sister. "I had this really strong sense that Daddy was there with me," I said. Tisha asked more questions about the details of the photo and frame than I could clearly explain, and I left the conversation unsure if she believed my story was real or imagined. I wasn't sure myself what was true.

In December, Tisha left her home in Maryland to return to Pittsburgh for Christmas. We were wrapping gifts in my upstairs sitting room when she brought up the incident of the picture frame.

"Show me what happened with the photo," she said.

I retrieved the silver frame from the hall table and brought it to her. "The photo was on an angle in the frame," I explained. "Here, I'll show you."

I removed the frame backing to place the picture on a diagonal, just as I found it that day in November. However, when I tried to turn the photo on an angle, it wouldn't fit. I examined the picture and matting and realized that the photograph was too big to fit on a diagonal in the frame. I could only get it to shift a minuscule amount, not nearly enough to be noticeable. After a few failed attempts to recreate the situation, I considered that maybe what I had experienced last month was a sign from my father.

I began to research accounts of such occurrences and discovered that reports of after-death communication—known as ADC—were not uncommon. Reports came from people of all ages, nationalities, incomes, education levels, and all religious affiliations. There were varied categories of experiences reported, such as sensing a physical presence as I had experienced, visions of the deceased, hearing a voice or feeling a touch, or even smelling an aroma associated with the dead like a familiar perfume.

There were also reports of physical phenomena similar to the photo of my grandmother Rose that appeared to have moved in its frame. Sometimes symbolic connections were associated with after-death communication with symbols such as pennies, birds, feathers, or butterflies.

I reluctantly shared the incident of the photo frame with my grown sons, telling them that I thought perhaps it was a sign from their grandfather. They placated me, saying, "If anyone could do it, Pops could." Yet, their side glances at each other and stifled smirks told me they were appeasing me. I chose not to disclose the occurrence with my mother, and she died without being aware of it. Mom was a devout Catholic and open to all things spiritual, and she would likely have embraced the event as divine. I'm not sure why I didn't tell her. Perhaps I didn't want to admit to her that I might have been wrong all those years ago. Still, looking back, it seems odd that I didn't share it with her.

After the incident with the picture frame, I started to dream about my dad. Once, I dreamed that I spotted him walking through a parking garage, rounding a corner several feet ahead of my car. I pulled the car over and jumped out, running towards him, calling, "Daddy, wait!" I turned the bend, and he was gone. In another dream, Dad appeared inside a subway car while I stood on the platform. I pounded on the door running beside the train as it pulled away. In each dream, Dad remained elusive, just out of reach. It felt like trying to grasp fog. Desperate to connect with Dad, I checked the picture frame often, hoping to find the photo skewed. It remained intact.

* * *

On a hot July afternoon in 2018, I pushed the stroller holding my four-year-old granddaughter up the long block before we turned onto my street. Alex and I were on our way home from the community swimming pool, where she had spent the last hour splashing in the kiddie pool fountain.

"Look, Nonna," Alex pointed to a spot high in front of her.

I didn't see what she was pointing to. "What is it?" I asked.

"A little butterfly. It's my friend."

I smiled at the notion that she found friendship with a butterfly.

"There, look!"

"I see it now," I said. A delicate white butterfly fluttered in front of Alex as we continued toward the house.

"It's following us!" she said with glee.

Indeed, the butterfly followed us to my front door and then seemed to linger on the porch after we went inside. Later, after lunch, Alex and I went into the backyard to play before she took her nap.

"Look, Nonna. My friend is here."

Sure enough, the small white butterfly danced over Alex's head. I watched as it seemed to follow her wherever she went in the yard as she played. Suddenly, I felt overwhelmed with thoughts of my mother. I had no idea what brought on this impulse, but I wondered if my mom was looking after Alex. I remember once Tisha saying that she thinks of our dad whenever she sees a red cardinal. I thought the notion ridiculous at the time but didn't say so. Now, there I was, associating my mother's spirit with a small white butterfly. I felt at once foolish yet somehow content.

While Alex took some notice of birds, squirrels, and other animals in the neighborhood, she seemed to have a special attachment to that butterfly. She named it "Jewel," and for the rest of the summer, Jewel was close by whenever Alex was visiting. I was pleased by Alex's bond with her butterfly friend. If it was a symbol of my mother, Mom certainly got the final word regarding the veracity of signs.

XIX

Decoration Day

I scooped Alex onto my lap so she could better view the old family photos on my computer screen. "Here's my mommy," I explained as we looked at a circa 1940s photo of my mom, wavy dark hair flowing to her shoulders, looking into the camera with a soft smile. "And here's my daddy." I pointed to a photo of my dad looking handsome in a suit and tie. It must have been a special occasion.

"Are they dead?" Alex asked. Her question surprised me.

"Yes, they're dead."

We turned to more recent photos. "Here's your daddy and Uncle Jason when they were little."

"And here's you, Nonna, when you had black hair!" She turned and stared at my hair, now mostly white with a few dark strands here and there. "And now you're old," she said.

I burst out laughing. This kid never failed to amuse me.

"And you're going to die," she stated in a matter-of-fact tone.

That comment shook me. Over the past five years, I'd faced the possibility of death. I'd had open heart surgery to repair a leaky valve. Recovery was challenging, and recuperation was slow but successful. The following year, doctors diagnosed me with cancer. The treatment was unforgiving and scary. But after months of chemotherapy, radiation, and a difficult surgery, I was cancer free. I'd confronted my own death and thought I'd moved beyond any anxiety attached to it, but Alex's comment unsettled me. Perhaps I wasn't past the fear of death. Or maybe I was afraid of losing the photographs, the memories, and the traditions, what felt like the substance of my life.

"Okay, enough with the pictures," I said as I slid her off my lap.

A few weeks later, Alex played on my office floor in front of the tall mahogany bookcases. She liked to study the book covers and look at the framed photos dotting the shelves.

"Here's my daddy!" she cried, pointing to a photo of Sean, as a teenager. "And here's you, Nonna!" She continued examining the pictures and stopped at one of my late husband. "Who's this?"

"That's your daddy's dad. His name was James, but we called him Jim." I didn't explain that my second husband, Jim, was not my sons' biological dad. "Remember I told you about how your middle name is for him? Alexandra James."

"Is he my grandfather?"

I was impressed that she figured this out so quickly. "Yes, baby girl. Good job!"

"Is he dead?" That question again.

"Yes, baby, he's dead."

A day or two later, I shared this incident on the phone with Jason. "She seems to have some fascination with people who are dead."

"Mom, have you taken Alex to the cemetery?"

"Heavens no. She's only four."

"But you took Sean and me when we were that little. You walked us from one grave to another and told the story of each person who was buried there."

Jason was right. I often took him and Sean to the cemetery when they were young. Later, when they were older, they helped me decorate each grave with flowers and repeated the stories I had shared with them.

After we hung up, I thought about a Saturday morning earlier in the year when Jason and I visited the cemetery together, preparing for Decoration Day. He carried the shovel and the flat of flowers, making his way from the road down the grassy hill. I followed with the trowel and watering can. "I can't remember if it's this row or the next," I yelled to him.

"I remember," he called back over his shoulder. And he always did. He knew exactly where each ancestor's grave was located. Using trees, statues, and headstones with memorable names as signposts, Jason worked his way through Mount Carmel Cemetery without a misstep.

***

Since it was established in 1889, Mount Carmel has served as the burial place for generations of Catholic families from the East End of Pittsburgh and the Eastern suburbs. Its fifty-three acres of grassy hills, trees, and pathways are the resting place for almost 28,000 deceased, most Italian-American.

Many of the deceased from Larimer Avenue, including my family, are buried in Mount Carmel. It's as though the Italian neighbors had abandoned their houses, grocery stores, and churches to gather again here on these grassy slopes. Mrs. Gentilcore, who owned the chicken store, is here, and our family friend Ursula who ran the beer store across from our apartment, is buried here. Damma Ciorra, our next-door neighbor on Larimer Avenue, is interned in the niche next to my mom and dad. Next-door neighbors for eternity.

I've been visiting my relatives at Mount Carmel for as long as I can remember. As a child, I spent the entire day there on Decoration Day with my parents, aunts, uncles, and cousins. In the days leading up to the Memorial Day holiday, Mom, Dad, Mim, and Uncle weeded, planted geraniums, and scrubbed headstones, ensuring each grave site was pristine. Several of our neighbors, also tending to the graves of their relatives, called and waved to each other as they worked. Then, on Decoration Day, we arrived early in the morning for the raising of the flag, followed by a 21-gun salute and a parade of veterans in uniform through the cemetery. My cousin Tommy and I would place a flag on each of the family grave sites. It didn't matter if the deceased were veterans. It was Decoration Day, so everyone got a flag. Sometimes, Uncle would take a photo of Tommy and me standing beside one of the headstones, holding our flags. Tommy is buried here at Mount Carmel now.

I've kept the tradition of visiting the cemetery every few months in the years since. Every spring, in preparation for Memorial Day, I come with Sean or Jason to weed, clean the headstones, plant flowers, and tell the stories of my ancestors. Czeslow Milosz, the Polish poet, said that "the living owe to those who no longer can speak to tell their story for them." I tell their stories.

My dad's mother, Rose Pape Schifino, is buried here with her twelve-year-old son, Samuel. My grandmother, Rose, died of influenza in 1919 when she was only twenty-nine, leaving four young children behind. I wished I had known her, this grandmother whose eyes I inherited, whose photo sits on my bookshelf. Her small headstone is weathered and worn, and I question if I'm accelerating the process by washing it each spring.

Rose's husband, my grandfather Angelo Schifino, is buried in an adjacent part of the cemetery. He died when my dad was ten, so I never knew him either. Once when Jason was about twelve, he and I were planting begonias in front of Angelo's grave. Suddenly, Jason stood.

"What the heck is with his first name? You told me that my middle name was for him. I can't believe I didn't see this before."

Jason's middle name is Andrew, and I explained that Angelo was always called Andrew or Andy, which I imagined was an attempt to Americanize. Jason was not at all satisfied, and for some time after, he referred to himself as Jason Angelo.

My great-grandfather, Urbano DeSantis, is buried just down the hillside from Angelo. Baw Baw was the only male ancestor alive when I was born, and I idolized him. Baw Baw, who had been legendary for his excessive drinking, sang Italian songs loudly in public and was ejected from the Italian Brotherhood Beneficial Association most nights for his unruly behavior. For some time after his burial, there was no grass on his grave. Dad and Uncle tried everything to encourage grass to grow—fertilizer, additional seed, frequent watering—but nothing worked. Finally, they gave up and planted sod. They liked telling everyone how Baw Baw was so ornery that grass refused to grow on his grave.

My mom's parents, Donato and Filomena Altieri, are buried together in a section near Baw Baw, marked by a stone with their photographs in small glass cases attached to the front. I didn't know my grandfather as he died long before I was born, but I was close with Grandma. I remember the smell of flour when I hugged her, watching her hands as she pressed pieces of dough into her kitchen table to make cavatelli and how her gold wedding band cut into her finger after sixty years, the softness of her voice, the comfort of her lap.

When Jason puts the first trowel slice into the dirt in front of Grandma's headstone each spring, I warn him not to go too deep. "I remember," he'd say. I've only shared the reason for this caution with Jason and Sean. I didn't want to broadcast that a plastic baggie with a small amount of my Aunt Gilda's cremated remains was buried in the dirt in front of her parent's headstone. When Gilda died while visiting Pittsburgh, her remains were returned to California with her children, where she had lived for many years. My mom wanted a piece of her sister to stay here at Mount Carmel with the family, so she secretly opened the urn that held the ashes, took a spoon from her kitchen drawer, and ladled out a bit of Aunt Gilda. Mom shared this with Mim and me but made us promise not to tell anyone. I can't imagine what the church would think, and I feared it might even have been illegal. Either way, at least a part of Aunt Gilda is here in Mount Carmel.

Mom and Dad, Mim and Uncle, and most of my ancestors rest here now with their relatives and friends—the Papes and the Perrinos, the Nardozzis, and the Martones—together in their perpetual neighborhood. Visiting their graves brings me joy. With each planting of a begonia, each watering, each cleaning of a headstone, they come alive again. I talk to them, asking for guidance, sharing stories about Alex, and expressing how much I miss them. I lace the tread, creating the continuum from them through me to Alex.

Late on a Friday afternoon at the height of the Coronavirus pandemic, I headed for the cemetery. I needed to talk with my parents and tell them that, for the first time, I felt ill-equipped to protect my family. Placing one hand on each niche, I rested my head against the cool marble and sobbed. I transferred my fear and put it in their hands. I visited my grandmother, Rose, and sat before her weathered stone pondering her death in another pandemic a century ago. I told her I was sorry and hoped she didn't die afraid or alone. I paused at the gravesites of my grandparents, aunts, uncles, great-grandfather, and my cousin Tommy. I stopped to say hello to Ursula. I laid hands on each headstone and whispered, "I love you." In the midst of social distancing and isolation, I found comfort in proximity to the dead. Mount Carmel has always been a place of solace for me—not for grieving, but for immersing myself in a community of ancestors, allowing them to swaddle me in love. The history of my people is buried in this place, their strengths, their wisdom. Mount Carmel is my neighborhood. I walked back to my car, letting the spring breeze cleanse me.

* * *

On the Saturday before Christmas. Alex and I approached the driveway entrance to Mount Carmel between the two stone pillars, each supporting a white marble statue, one of Jesus with his arms outstretched and the other of his mother, Mary. We pulled into a parking space in front of the Saint John of the Cross Mausoleum, where multicolored stained-glass windows curve gracefully over the etched glass entrance doors. Inside, the deceased are entombed in crypts along each side wall with benches down the center of the chamber for visitors. Cremated remains are interned in niches lining the outside walls of the mausoleum. This is where my parents rest.

I reached for the small pieces of evergreen tied with red ribbons I brought from home, gathered Alex from her car seat, and headed to the outside wall. "Here's where we come to visit my mom and daddy," I explained as I carefully placed the evergreen in the little brass vases attached to the front of their niches. "See, these are their names."

"Who are all these other people?" she asked, pointing to photos affixed to the outside of several surrounding niches. "Are they dead too?"

"Yes. Everyone here is dead." I didn't tell her I had already arranged for a niche for myself above the ones holding my parents. We stood for a few minutes, Alex wandering from photo to photo, studying the faces of the deceased and me gazing at my parents' names, remembering their faces, the sound of their voices, and their touch. Alex needs to know these people, memorialize them, and give meaning to their lives. I realized at this moment that this was why I'd brought her here so that she would someday put sprigs of evergreen in the brass vase beside my name.

I turned to Alex. "Do you want to see Mim's grave? You remember she's the one who taught me the songs I teach you." I took her small hand and walked several yards to Mim and Uncle's grave. I reached down with my glove and cleaned leaves and dead grass from the granite marker I had selected for them some years ago. Then, Alex and I sang one of the songs that Mim taught me: "Barefoot Days," Alex's favorite. Our voices rang out, cutting through the stillness.

When we headed back to the car, I noticed a small deer resting under a tree at the driveway's edge. It didn't flinch as we approached, and I realized it might be sick or hurt. At the very least, it was lost, as no other deer were in sight. I was distressed for the baby deer, seemingly abandoned in this quiet place—such a contrast to Alex and me, surrounded by our loved ones.

As we approached the car, I promised Alex that we'd return. "We'll come back when the weather is warmer and visit more relatives."

"Can we sing?" she asked.

"Yes, baby girl, we can sing."

XX

Epilogue – Spaces Filled

March 2021

I zipped my favorite wool sweater, the pretty aqua one I bought in Dublin, to add one more layer, grabbed my purse and face mask, and got in my Honda. Two weeks after my second Covid vaccine, I needed to be out in the world. Like many others, I'd spent the past year shopping online, picking up groceries and meals curbside, and visiting with family and friends on Zoom. Full vaccination became the get-out-of-jail-free card that allowed me and many of my generation to see our grandchildren again inside, without masks, hugging. Alex's sleepover this past weekend was my gift—a celebration in exchange for a year of patience (well, mostly patience) and extreme care. Now, I headed out to the second reward on my list—the Strip District.

The Strip seemed quiet, with few shoppers on the street, and I found a parking space on Penn Avenue, the main drag, where there were still delivery trucks at 10:00 A.M. My first stop was Pennsylvania Macaroni, or Penn Mac, the largest Italian grocery in the Strip. I picked up a small bottle of balsamic vinegar and a package of penne pasta, then made my way through the narrow aisles to the cheese counter where Ursula had worked years ago. A tall, thin young man with a shock of brown hair peeking out from his cap greeted me, and I asked for a piece of imported provolone. I was impressed with his familiarity with the large selection of cheeses, pointing to special varieties and explaining the differences in taste and texture. He recommended a provolone *piccante* for its sharp flavor, offering me a sample. Aged to savory perfection, the *piccante* tasted spicy and a bit salty on my tongue. I added the cheese to my basket and headed for the register.

Outside, I crossed the street and walked down Penn Avenue toward Wholey's, the pinnacle of all things fish and seafood. My mask hid the smiles I shared with the occasional stranger I encountered on the sidewalk. I liked to think that they smiled back. The Strip seemed unusually calm, but once inside Wholey's, the energy picked up with the buzz of conversation from customers in line along the extensive fresh fish station. There were rows of refrigerated cases stacked high with shrimp, crab legs, octopus, whole red snapper and trout, grouper filets, and swordfish steaks. When it was my turn, I asked the woman behind the counter to hold up one salmon filet after another until I was satisfied, just like Mim had taught me.

My last stop was Sunseri's, where I was the only customer. I had been looking forward to seeing Jimmy, his familiar unlit cigar jutting from the side of his mouth, but he wasn't in his usual spot behind the counter. Instead, a young woman wearing a Steelers t-shirt stood at the register. The store smelled of olive brine, cheese, and baked goods. I stopped to scoop black olives from a barrel into a plastic container and picked up a loaf of crusty Italian bread from a shelf. Then, I moved on to the pastry case and selected one *sfogliatelle*.

Once outside, the quiet of the street matched the solitude of the pandemic. Yet, I found contentment in remembering the once-happy rhythm of this place, knowing that it would come alive again. As I returned to my car, I knew where I wanted to go next.

My Larimer Avenue neighborhood has changed in the past four years. I started my drive down Meadow Street, knowing that Our Lady Help of Christians had been torn down over a year ago. Still, I wanted to see the site. I pictured what might remain—a few steps, some familiar yellow bricks, perhaps the remnant of one of the gold domes. Unrecognizable, I almost missed where my family's church once stood. I parked across from a gravel parking lot, neatly maintained, with rows of cars parked inside a new-looking fence. There was no trace of the church. The former Help of Christians Elementary School building remained behind the parking lot, repurposed as the Urban Academy of Greater Pittsburgh. The building looked clean and well-preserved, an improvement over the original. I left with an unexpectedly positive feeling.

I turned my Honda toward Larimer Avenue and my old school. I read recently that the building was sold to a developer who planned to convert it into apartments. I found a construction site at the corner of Larimer and Shetland. A bulldozer stood in the front yard, and two dump trucks sat on the street in front of the school. Men in bright yellow vests directed the few cars that passed around the construction vehicles. Across from the school, a new wrought iron fence surrounded the old club yard, newly populated with park benches and playground equipment atop an expanse of green grass. It looked fresh and somehow uplifting. Next to the club yard, a basketball court with a new surface and fence waited for players. I thought to myself that all Larimer Avenue needs now are people who are neighbors.

Further down Larimer toward the last block before the bridge. I stopped in front of Henry Grasso's store and peeked through the window. I could see lights on and two men working, and I suddenly wanted to be inside talking with them. I parked in the lot beside the store, what used to be Gentilcore's coal yard, and headed toward the front entrance. When I opened the makeshift plywood outer door, I saw someone reach for the inner door and heard a lock click. Inside, Grasso's looked very different and much smaller than I remembered all those years ago. The floor was covered in a white vinyl tile that I'm sure had long ago replaced the sawdust. The glass-enclosed meat cases were gone. One long white porcelain table extended from front to back along the center of the small store, and a counter with a scale and cash register ran along the right wall. Two men worked, faces masked, heads covered with hair nets. One stood at the far end of the porcelain table, arranging long sausage rings into large plastic bags that he tied at the top when filled, while the other stood behind the counter weighing sausage and packaging it in white paper. They didn't look up when I came in. I had come for a conversation but knew I first needed to be a customer.

After a few moments, the man behind the counter asked if he could help me. I ordered two pounds of sweet Italian sausage and asked that they be packaged separately. I planned to deliver a pound to each of my sons. I mentioned that I hadn't been in this store in years. No reaction from either man. "I used to live two doors away," I said. The man behind the long table briefly glanced up.

"You used to live here on Larimer?"

"Yeah, two doors away upstairs from Mr. Corazza's grocery store."

"I remember Corazza's store," he said without looking up.

"I'm Linda," I introduced myself. He didn't respond, so I ventured a guess. "Are you related to Mr. Grasso?"

"I'm his son, Joe," he replied, head down, not interrupting his work.

"And I'm Jim, his brother-in-law," the man behind the register chimed in as he weighed my sausage order and told me about their other products: hot and Sicilian sausages, salami, and *soppressata*.

Both men seemed polite, but I realized I hadn't engaged them yet. Not enough to ask all the questions that had been swimming in my head for years: did Joe remember the IBBA, the coal yard, Ursula's store? Why were some buildings numbered 600 and some 700 in the same block? So many questions. I made another attempt.

"I remember your father and this store," I told Joe. I began to describe the sawdust floor, the barrels of olives, and the plastic pig that hung on the wall behind where Mr. Grasso worked. When I mentioned the plastic pig, Joe's hands stopped, he looked up, and his dark eyes connected with mine for the first time.

"You remember that pig?" I detected a smile beneath his mask. I saw it in the crinkle around his eyes. I realized that I had just earned my credibility with Joe Grasso.

Joe and I spent the next several minutes in animated conversation, about my mom buying pickled pig's feet, about Mr. Corazza's store, about the drunks leaving the IBBA at 5:00 A.M. when Joe and his dad arrived at work. Like me, he never figured out the crazy street numbering on this block. Both excited to make this connection, we welcomed sharing our own memories with someone else who remembered. Yet, Joe didn't only look back; he spoke of his hopes for the future of the neighborhood. We talked about the apartments going into the school building, and Joe said, "You know, people from Google might move here." I didn't tell him that I didn't want to see the neighborhood gentrified or that I was happy to have read that the apartments would be mixed-use funded by a HUD grant. Yet, I was grateful to Joe for his optimism, forward thinking, and recognition that Larimer Avenue was a living neighborhood encompassing more than its past. Joe's vision inspired me to imagine Larimer as a home for future neighborhood girls who might, like Alex, have a connection to this former Italian American enclave. I pictured a vibrant Larimer Avenue, a robust community with stores and shoppers, children playing in the club yard, and a new generation of neighbors creating families and memories. I felt content and hopeful.

"I'm glad you're still here," I told Joe.

"Where do you live now?" he asked. When I told him Squirrel Hill, Joe said, "That's close. Come back again, okay?" I promised him I'd return, knowing that I would.

I left the store with two pounds of sausage and a full heart, giddy, simultaneously laughing and crying. On my drive home, I thought about the genealogy research I had done during the pandemic, tracing Grandma's ancestors back to the early 1700s in Castelluccio Valmaggiore, a little town in the Province of Foggia. I wondered about their customs, their food, and what they valued, and I realized that my family traditions didn't start or end here. Our family history didn't begin with Grandma, Mom and Dad, Mim and Uncle here in the Larimer Avenue neighborhood or the Strip District, and it wouldn't end here. It didn't matter how many fishes we ate on Christmas Eve or what songs we sang. It mattered that we ate and sang together.

I headed home and drove past the new playground again. I thought maybe I'd bring Alex here, sit on a bench while I watched her swing and slide, and tell her stories of my childhood.

Epilogue – Spaces Filled 147

Henry Grasso's store on Larimer Avenue, 2023.

About the Author

LINDA SCHIFINO is a writer living in Pittsburgh. She holds a Ph.D. in rhetoric from Duquesne University and an MFA in Creative Nonfiction from Carlow University, where she is also Professor Emerita of Communication. Linda is a longtime writer with Madwomen in the Attic, a diverse community of serious women writers who offer each other support and share their love of the written word. She also teaches writing through the Osher Lifelong Learning Institute at Carnegie Mellon University.

As the eldest member of her immediate family, Linda is the keeper of family memories and traditions. When she retired from academia, Linda began writing essays about growing up in an Italian American enclave in 1950s Pittsburgh to preserve her family's memories and as a salve to her painful loss of people and community. These essays later evolved into *Neighborhood Girl*. Linda's current writing project has taken her to a small village in southern Italy to investigate her ancestry and the mysteries surrounding the life of her maternal great-grandmother.

Schifino has published essays in *Adelaide Magazine, Avalon Literary Journal, Brevity Blog, Northern Appalachia Review, The Write Launch*, and elsewhere. When she's not writing, Linda spends time in her garden, at dance class, and reading. She also loves playing with her granddaughter, Alex, and exploring her Squirrel Hill neighborhood with her dog, Lizzie.

You can find Linda on Facebook at Linda Schifino | Facebook
on Instagram at Linda Schifino (@lindaschifino)
and on her website lindaschifino.com

Printed in the USA
CPSIA information can be obtained
at www.ICGtesting.com
JSHW032302290823
47518JS00004B/180